JUVENILE

CENTRAL

MYSTERIES, LEGENDS, AND UNEXPLAINED PHENOMENA

FAIRIES

MYSTERIES, LEGENDS, AND UNEXPLAINED PHENOMENA

MYSTERIES, LEGENDS, AND UNEXPLAINED PHENOMENA

FAIRIES

ROSEMARY ELLEN GUILEY

Consulting Editor: Rosemary Ellen Guiley

CHELSEA HOUSE
PUBLISHERS
An imprint of Infobase Publishing

FAIRIES

Chelsea House
An imprint of Infobase Publishing
132 West 31st Street
New York NY 10001

Library of Congress Cataloging-in-Publication Data

Guiley, Rosemary.
    Fairies / Rosemary Ellen Guiley.
        p. cm. — (Mysteries, legends, and unexplained phenomena)
    Includes bibliographical references (p.   ) and index.
    ISBN-13: 978-1-60413-630-2 (alk. paper)
    ISBN-10: 1-60413-630-8 (alk. paper)
  1. Fairies. I. Title. II. Series.

    BF1552.G85 2010
    398'.45—dc22   2009026018

Chelsea House books are available at special discounts when purchased in bulk quantities for businesses, associations, institutions, or sales promotions. Please call our Special Sales Department in New York at (212) 967-8800 or (800) 322-8755.

You can find Chelsea House on the World Wide Web at http://www.chelseahouse.com

Text design by James Scotto-Lavino
Cover design by Ben Peterson
Composition by EJB Publishing Services
Cover printed by Bang Printing, Brainerd, MN
Book printed and bound by Bang Printing, Brainerd, MN
Date printed: November, 2009
Printed in the United States of America

10 9 8 7 6 5 4 3 2 1

This book is printed on acid-free paper.

All links and Web addresses were checked and verified to be correct at the time of publication. Because of the dynamic nature of the Web, some addresses and links may have changed since publication and may no longer be valid.

Contents

Foreword

Did you ever have an experience that turned your whole world upside down? Maybe you saw a ghost or a UFO. Perhaps you had an unusual, vivid dream that seemed real. Maybe you suddenly knew that a certain event was going to happen in the future. Or, perhaps you saw a creature or a being that did not fit the description of anything known in the natural world. At first you might have thought your imagination was playing tricks on you. Then, perhaps, you wondered about what you experienced and went looking for an explanation.

Every day and night people have experiences they can't explain. For many people these events are life changing. Their comfort zone of what they can accept as "real" is put to the test. It takes only one such experience for people to question the reality of the mysterious worlds that might exist beyond the one we live in. Perhaps you haven't encountered the unknown, but you have an intense curiosity about it. Either way, by picking up this book, you've started an adventure to explore and learn more, and you've come to the right place! The book you hold has been written by a leading expert in the paranormal—someone who understands unusual experiences and who knows the answers to your questions.

As a seeker of knowledge, you have plenty of company. Mythology, folklore, and records of the past show that human beings have had paranormal experiences throughout history. Even prehistoric cave paintings and gravesites indicate that early humans had concepts of the supernatural and of an afterlife. Humans have always sought to understand paranormal experiences and to put them into a frame of reference that makes sense to us in our daily lives. Some of the greatest minds in history have grappled with questions about the paranormal. For example, Greek philosopher Plato pondered the nature of dreams and how we "travel" during them. Isaac Newton was interested in the esoteric study of alchemy, which has magical elements, and St. Thomas Aquinas explored the nature of angels and spirits. Philosopher William James joined organizations dedicated to psychical research; and even the inventor of the light bulb, Thomas Alva Edison, wanted to build a device that could talk to the dead. More recently, physicists such as David Bohm, Stephen Hawking, William Tiller, and Michio Kaku have developed ideas that may help explain how and why paranormal phenomena happen, and neuroscience researchers like Michael Persinger have explored the nature of consciousness.

Exactly what is a paranormal experience or phenomenon? "Para" is derived from a Latin term for "beyond." So "paranormal" means "beyond normal," or things that do not fit what we experience through our five senses alone and which do not follow the laws we observe in nature and in science. Paranormal experiences and phenomena run the gamut from the awesome and marvelous, such as angels and miracles, to the downright terrifying, such as vampires and werewolves.

Paranormal experiences have been consistent throughout the ages, but explanations of them have changed as societies, cultures, and technologies have changed. For example, our ancestors were much closer to the invisible realms. In times when life was simpler, they saw, felt, and experienced other realities on a daily basis. When night fell, the darkness was thick and quiet, and it was easier to see unusual things, such as ghosts. They had no electricity to keep the night lit up. They had no media for constant communication and entertainment. Travel was difficult. They had more time to notice subtle things that were just beyond their ordinary senses. Few doubted their experiences. They accepted the invisible realms as an extension of ordinary life.

Today, we have many distractions. We are constantly busy, from the time we wake up until we go to bed. The world is full of light and noise 24 hours a day, seven days a week. We have television, the Internet, computer games, and cell phones to keep us busy, busy, busy.

We are ruled by technology and science. Yet, we still have paranormal experiences very similar to those of our ancestors. Because these occurrences do not fit neatly into science and technology, many people think they are illusions, and there are plenty of skeptics always ready to debunk the paranormal and reinforce that idea.

In roughly the past 100 years, though, some scientists have studied the paranormal and attempted to find scientific evidence for it. Psychic phenomena have proven difficult to observe and measure according to scientific standards. However, lack of scientific proof does not mean paranormal experiences do not happen. Courageous scientists are still looking for bridges between science and the supernatural.

My personal experiences are behind my lifelong study of the paranormal. Like many children I had invisible playmates when I was very young, and I saw strange lights in the yard and woods that I instinctively knew were the nature spirits who lived there. Children seem to be very open to paranormal phenomena, but their ability to have these experiences often fades away as they become more involved in the outside world, or, perhaps, as adults tell them not to believe in what they experience, that it's only in their imagination. Even when I was very young, I was puzzled that other people would tell me with great authority that I did not experience what I knew I did.

A major reason for my interest in the paranormal is precognitive dreaming experienced by members of my family. Precognition means "fore knowing," or knowing the future. My mother had a lot of psychic experiences, including dreams of future events. As a teen it seemed amazing to me that dreams could show us the future. I was determined to learn more about this and to have such dreams myself. I found books that explained extrasensory perception, the knowing of information beyond the five senses. I learned about dreams and experimented with them. I taught myself to visit distant places in my dreams and to notice details about them that I could later verify in the physical world. I learned how to send people telepathic messages in dreams and how to receive messages in dreams. Every night became an exciting adventure.

Those interests led me to other areas of the paranormal. Pretty soon I was engrossed in studying all kinds of topics. I learned different techniques for divination, including the Tarot. I learned how to meditate. I took courses to develop my own psychic skills, and I gave psychic readings to others. Everyone has at least some natural psychic ability and can improve it with attention and practice.

Next I turned my attention to the skies, to ufology, and what might be "out there" in space. I studied the lore of angels and fairies. I delved into the dark shadowy realm of demons and monsters. I learned the principles of real magic and spell casting. I undertook investigations of haunted places. I learned how to see auras and do energy healing. I even participated in some formal scientific laboratory experiments for telepathy.

My studies led me to have many kinds of experiences that have enriched my understanding of the paranormal. I cannot say that I can prove anything in scientific terms. It may be some time yet before science and the paranormal stop flirting with each other and really get together. Meanwhile, we can still learn a great deal from our personal experiences. At the very least, our paranormal experiences contribute to our inner wisdom. I encourage others to do the same as I do. Look first for natural explanations of strange phenomena. If natural explanations cannot be found or seem unlikely, consider paranormal explanations. Many paranormal experiences fall into a vague area, where although natural causes might exist, we simply don't know what could explain them. In that case I tell people to trust their intuition that they had a paranormal experience. Sometimes the explanation makes itself known later on.

I have concluded from my studies and experiences that invisible dimensions are layered upon our world, and that many paranormal experiences occur when there are openings between worlds. The doorways often open at unexpected times. You take a trip, visit a haunted place, or have a strange dream—and suddenly reality shifts. You get a glimpse behind the curtain that separates the ordinary from the extraordinary.

The books in this series will introduce you to these exciting and mysterious subjects. You'll learn many things that will astonish you. You'll be given lots of tips for how to explore the paranormal on your own. Paranormal investigation is a popular field, and you don't have to be a scientist or a full-time researcher to explore it. There are many things you can do in your free time. The knowledge you gain from these books will help prepare you for any unusual and unexpected experiences.

As you go deeper into your study of the paranormal, you may come up with new ideas for explanations. That's one of the appealing aspects of paranormal investigation—there is always room for bold ideas. So, keep an open and curious mind, and think big. Mysterious worlds are waiting for you!

—Rosemary Ellen Guiley

Introduction

*O*f all the supernatural beings familiar to humans, fairies are among the most intriguing. They seem very much like people but yet are wildly different. They share the planet but have their own secret domain. They interact with people on their own terms.

Fairies have puzzled humans for centuries. They have eluded attempts to know more about them, so for the most part they have been left alone and thought of as something to fear. Throughout history people have left written and oral accounts of strange little folk dancing jigs in the moonlight or buzzing like human bees around flowers and plants, and wreaking havoc when they were displeased with people. These accounts have shaped contemporary thoughts about fairies. In the modern, high-tech world, fairies seem outmoded and out of place, something cute in a fairy-tale book that people "back when" imagined.

Fairies are in need of a new image, and they are getting a makeover in popular thought. An increasing number of people acknowledge contact with fairies and want to know more about them. Fairy art, books, and festivals celebrate and explore these mysterious beings. Instead of being elusive, fairies have increasingly come forward, not only to make themselves known to people, but also to enter into working relationships with them. These relationships often center around environmental activities that aid nature.

Most of the experiences that humans have involving beings not of this reality are spontaneous and rare. For example, few people ever encounter a Bigfoot or a winged humanoid. Even encounters with angels and aliens are not the stuff of daily life and certainly do not occur "on demand."

Yet fairies are everywhere all the time. With a bit of practice and persistence, most people can learn to see them, and perhaps even to communicate with them.

Like many young children, I had invisible playmates. They looked like me, and they joined me usually when I was entertaining myself with toys and games. Adults who hear of these playmates pass them off as the product of a vivid imagination, but children may actually be playing with fairies, which have a long tradition of attraction to young humans. The playmates go away as children get older and become more absorbed in the physical world. The fairies move on and look for new children who can see and accept them without question.

Over the years I have had other experiences of fairies. I didn't go looking for them but had spontaneous experiences that made me wonder about the true nature and reality of fairies. While living in a house in a woodsy area, I noticed small lights moving among the trees, especially at dusk. Were they natural phenomena? In fairy lore, bobbing lights are a common form that fairies take.

I spent years developing psychic and intuitive skills, and learned how to shift my vision so that other realities became unveiled. I found I could see the lights at will, and even establish mental contact with the intelligence behind them.

Still, fairies seem to maintain the upper hand. They can keep themselves invisible, or they can appear to people they like. They have a long tradition of this behavior, too. They respond to people who have a serious interest in them and a respectful approach.

Once I was traveling around England and visited the site of the ruins of a Roman dream temple, Lydney, located near the border of Wales. Dream temples were used in ancient times for healing. Pilgrims went to the temple in the hopes that healing gods would visit them in dreams and cure them of their ailments.

The ruins were located in a wild place on a hilltop, a place still charged with strange energies. I had heard that the fairy presence was

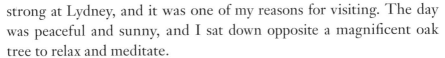

strong at Lydney, and it was one of my reasons for visiting. The day was peaceful and sunny, and I sat down opposite a magnificent oak tree to relax and meditate.

Presently I became aware that someone was looking at me; it was a little man about two feet high. He seemed to come out of the oak tree roots. He stood by the tree regarding me with curiosity. He had whiskers or a beard and a little red cap perched on his head. I was startled but did not move, lest I break what seemed like a magical spell. I mentally sent him a greeting and got one back. It seemed he just wanted to check me out, having caught my "vibe" of interest in fairies. He then disappeared, and I had the impression that he slid back down into the earth via the tree roots. Back to Fairyland he went!

There were other experiences as well. Once the door was opened to fairies, more of them came through. Upon my return to the United States, I became aware that I had a resident in my yard and house. It was another little fellow who looked human-like, but whose skin and hair seemed to be made out of leaves, twigs, and bark. I had the impression that he belonged to the yard, but he liked to slip into the house. Sometimes visitors to my house could see him, too. When I moved, he stayed behind. He was tied to the land, not to me.

Most of people's experiences with fairies occur in nature, which is their favored environment. But fairies can be encountered in houses and buildings, too. And, they can be encountered during meditative states. Fairies are nonlocal, that is, they exist in an otherworldly realm that operates under different rules and conditions than our physical reality. Fairies can make themselves known anywhere.

Exploring the world of fairies is both enlightening and fun. The folklore about them is fascinating: fairies are mysterious, powerful, and even dangerous at times. But the times have changed, and people are seeking positive experiences and relationships with fairies.

Where did fairies originate? Were they always on the planet? Did they get here before humans? People have long pondered these questions and have come up with various explanations. Chapter 1, "The Mysterious Origins of Fairies," explores those ideas. Despite the best attempts to dig out the answers, much about fairies remain shrouded in mystery.

Chapter 2, "Meet the Fairies," makes introductions to some of the best-known fairies. Their appearances, behaviors, and abilities are described. Fairies do not belong only to the past. They are the invisible playmates of children and the constant attendants of nature.

Fairies live in a world parallel to the mortal realm. In earlier times, this was perceived as being underground, accessed through a mound or hill. Humans were forbidden access, but sometimes stumbled upon it, or were invited by fairies. The mound may symbolize an unseen door to another dimension. Today, these doorways, or portals, are believed to exist in places around the world. They are interfaces between our realm and other dimensions. Chapter 3, "Where Fairies Live," describes what people have experienced when they visited Fairyland.

Chapter 4, "The Life of Fairies," tells about how fairies spend their time. Like humans, they have families and live and work in communities. Most of them are happy all the time, and enjoy themselves immensely in dance, music, and entertainment. In some respects, Fairyland is a strange mirror of human life, and perhaps represents the life people wish they had.

Fairies may seem like humans in many respects, but they have superpowers most people do not. Chapter 5, "Fairy Powers," talks about their psychic and supernormal abilities and powers, and the ways that fairies use them to influence people.

Chapter 6, "Bad Fairies," explores the darker side of the fairy realm. Human beings range in temperament from nice to nasty and so do fairies. Some like to play tricks on people, and some are outright mean and malevolent.

Chapter 7, "Changelings" discusses the fascination fairies have with human babies. They kidnap infants and leave behind their own undesired babies. Are there natural explanations? In the past fairies may have been blamed for sudden death in infants.

Fairies are not unique in human experience. They share many similarities with other mysterious beings, most notably extraterrestrials, which are discussed in Chapter 8, "The Extraterrestrial Connection." Is it an accident that the ETs encountered in modern times, and the abductions, enchantments, missing time, and other behaviors associated with them, mirror the fairies of earlier times? Folklorists and ufologists have raised intriguing questions that have yet to be answered.

Chapter 9, "How to See Fairies," covers ways to see and communicate with fairies. In earlier times, only certain people could see fairies: witches, wizards, sorcerers, prophets, and others who were born with "the sight," or clairvoyance, the ability to see the unseen. Sometimes the fairies took a liking to a certain person and gave him or her the sight. Today we know that anyone can learn to see fairies by training the senses to a subtle awareness. Also, more fairies may now wish to be seen and have come forward to work with people.

Chapter 10, "Enchanted Gardens, Enchanted World," discusses ideas for an active partnership between the fairy realm and the human realm. Intentional communities such as Findhorn and Green Hope Farm have demonstrated that a working relationship between the two realms leads to benefits for the environment, the planet, and enlightened consciousness among humans. People can participate in this evolution on their own, right in their homes and backyards. Fairies offer much more than only a supernatural experience; they offer the possibility of a new world awareness.

The Mysterious Origins of Fairies

In twelfth-century England, the villagers in tiny Woolpit, Suffolk, worried about wolves attacking their livestock. Today, the wolf is extinct in England, but back then, packs of them roamed the forests. Livestock made easy meals, and occasionally wolves attacked people, too. The residents of Woolpit dug deep pits to trap the wolves.

One day they caught something strange in the pits: not wolves, but two children, a boy and a girl. They looked like humans, but they had green skin. They couldn't communicate in any known language.

The puzzled villagers took the frightened green children to the local knight, Sir Richard de Cain. The boy and girl wept bitterly. They indicated they were hungry, but refused to eat the bread and meat offered to them. At last the villagers figured out that they would eat beans and nothing else.

In a short while the boy declined in health and died. The girl recovered and eventually learned to speak English. She told the villagers that she and the boy came from a place called St. Martin's Land, lit by a perpetual light like sunset. They were out tending their flocks when they encountered a cavern and heard the sound of bells. They followed the sounds and came out the mouth of the cavern. They were immediately struck senseless by the brilliant and intense light of earthly sun and the heavy temperature of the air. They lay unable to move for a long time and were unable to flee when the people arrived.

The girl entered into the service of the knight. She eventually married and never returned to her native land. The villagers were never able to find the mysterious cavern or opening that linked their world, the Land Above, to the world of the Green Children, the Land Below. The boy and girl remained a mystery, the fairies that came to earth.

The story is recorded in several sources, with some variations of detail. The green skin color, the everlasting twilight, and the underground land are consistent with many accounts of fairies, mysterious beings who share the earth with mortals.[1]

Since ancient times human beings have been aware of the possibility that they may share the planet with strange or magical beings that live in nature, the elements, and underground. Many of them look like humans, and many more are strange creatures of different shapes and sizes. Some of them seem to be part human and part animal, and others seem to be made of the stuff of trees and bushes. They have supernatural powers, which they will not hesitate to use against people when angry or displeased. People have learned that it is wise not to cross fairies and to give them plenty of respect.

Most of what is known about fairies in Western culture comes from Celtic lore in Ireland, Scotland, England, the Isle of Man, France, and parts of Europe. Fairies are found everywhere around the world, however, but they are known by different names. No matter what they are called, they are similar in appearances and characteristics, and they do the same things.

The term *fairy* comes from the Latin word *fata*, or fate.[2] In Greek mythology, the Fates are three women who spin, twist, and cut the threads of life. In medieval usage, "fairy" referred to women who had magical powers and could create a state of enchantment. The strange folk seen by humans also had the powers of enchantment. They became prominent characters in many folk tales and legends, which are known as fairy tales. Fairy tales are not only for children, but entertain and teach lessons to people of all ages.

WHERE DO FAIRIES COME FROM?

The origins of fairies are lost in time. In some accounts, even the fairies themselves do not know where their ancestors came from, except that fairies races are older than humans and were on earth first.[3]

Since there are many types of fairies, there probably is no one origin that fits them all. Some may be **nature spirits** that were created along with the natural world. Others may be residents of parallel dimensions that are close to earth. Others may be associated with the souls of human dead or may have distant, ancestral connections to humans.

Some people think that fairies are a type of angel. This belief has arisen because popular images of fairies show them with wings. Fairies, however, are not angels, and few descriptions of them include wings. Some fairies tend to things in nature the way some angels look after people, but the similarity ends there. Fairies and angels each have their own domain.

Explanations of fairies and their origins have varied throughout history to reflect changing beliefs about the world. Fairy lore is much older than Christianity, but some of it in the West has acquired Christian elements. And, since the development of modern ufology, fairies have been compared to extraterrestrials, and thought by some to have off-planet origins, an idea that will be explored later in this book.

There are several major explanations for the origins of fairies.

Fairies Are Small Human Beings

The dominant explanation for fairies in Celtic folklore is that they are an old, primitive race of humans that went into hiding in order to survive. In some accounts, the early fairies were gentle and peace loving and were no match for the brutal, bloodthirsty humans who arrived later on the earth. In self-defense, the fairies retreated more and more into remote areas, until they finally went underground and vanished altogether.

The most famous legends of fairy origins concern the Tuatha de Danaan (pronounced *tootha day danan*) of Ireland. The Tuatha de

Danaan were the children of the mother goddess Dana (also called Danu). They came to Ireland and conquered the Firbolgs (*fir vulag*), the original inhabitants of the land. The Firbolgs were forced to retreat to the Western Islands, where they became the first fairies, ugly giants.

The Tuatha de Danaan were themselves conquered by a race called the Milesians. They, too, were forced to retreat to the West, taking shelter under grassy mounds and under water. The Tuatha de Danaan were skilled in magic and used their abilities to hide from their conquerors. They became fairies, the Daoine Sidhe (*theena shee*).

One of the places that became their new home is the mystical land Tír Na nÓg or Tirnanog (*teer na nogue*), "The Land of the Young." Tír Na nÓg lies across the Western Sea, a paradise of pleasures and delights where time passes much more slowly than it does in the land of humans. The Sidhe live gracious lives like medieval royalty, knights, and ladies. Mortals have no access to this land, except when fairies kidnap them or invite them, or they accidentally stumble upon a magical doorway.

Other legends of little people who turned into fairies swirl around real **dwarf** or pygmy humans. There is ample evidence that small races of people have existed. According to lore, they live in wild, secret places and keep to themselves. Small skeletal remains and tiny tools and arrowheads have been found in many countries.[4]

Are these small races actually ordinary but primitive humans or supernatural fairies? Their factual existence blurs with legend, in which some of them are said to have magical powers and to be invisible most of the time.

Sightings of small, human-like beings have been recorded for centuries, even into modern times. For example, numerous encounters with dwarfs about two feet in height were recorded throughout Europe. They lived in cellars, tried to steal human babies, and even conversed with people. In 1975 school children on the island of Fiji in the South Pacific Ocean said they saw hairy little dwarfs about two feet in height. The creatures showed their teeth and ran away when

Figure 1.1 *A gnome, an earth elemental, enjoys a candlelit meal in his cave.* (C. Walker/Topham/The Image Works)

the children approached them. Though threatened with punishment, the children stuck to their stories.[5]

Fairies Are Nature Spirits

Early human beings believed the natural world was animated by living beings that managed the forces of nature and made things grow and die. These views are still popular with some people today. Nature spirits and **elementals** (beings connected to the four elements) are often included in fairy lore. They are usually invisible, have different forms associated with their roles in nature, and are more interested in their duties in nature than in interacting with human beings.

Earth elementals include small, human-like beings such as gnomes, pigmies, and **kobolds**. They take care of mines, caves, vegetation, forests, and gardens. Their clothing or even their skin may seem like leaves and tree bark.

Water elementals include undines and nymphs, beautiful watery beings (often female) that live in lakes, ponds, streams, and other bodies of water. Some, like the **kelpies** of Scottish Highlands lore, are tricksters or evil and like to lure people into waters and drown them.

Fire elementals include salamanders, lizard-like beings that thrive in flames.[6]

Air elementals feature sylphs, who govern the wind and weather and cause storms to arise. Sylphs are wispy, like streams of air.

According to lore, those elementals that have more human-like forms can mate with humans and produce hybrid offspring.

Fairies Come from Parallel Worlds

Humans have had many encounters with strange beings throughout history, giving weight to the idea that there are parallel, inhabited worlds and doorways that connect them to this world. For the most part, the worlds remain separate, but sometimes doors or windows spring open. In folklore, the doorways open more easily during certain

Fairies by Any Other Name

Fairies have many nicknames given to them by people. The nicknames are not given out of fondness for fairies the way people give affectionate nicknames to each other. Rather, the nicknames are intended to pacify fairies so that they will not trouble people. According to lore, fairies do not like the term *fairy* and prefer other names.

Since fairies are invisible, a person never knows when they might be around eavesdropping. Therefore, it is wise to always speak of them in a favorable voice and with kind words and terms for them. The Good Neighbors, the Good People, and the Gentry are three of the most common nicknames for fairies. They are also called

- The Fair Folk
- The Forgetful People
- The Hill Folk
- The Honest Folk
- Their Mother's Blessing
- The Men of Peace
- The Mob
- The People of Peace
- The People of That Town
- The Silent Moving Folk

Fairies also are known as the Little People, the L'il Fellas, and the Little Folk, but by some accounts, some fairies consider those terms disrespectful. On the Isle of Man it is considered especially dangerous and unlucky to use the term *fairy*. The preferred terms there are Themselves, They, and Them That's In It.

Figure 1.2 *The salamander is a fire elemental. It eats fire and chooses to live in the flames.* (C. Walker/Topfoto/The Image Works)

times of the year. Legends say that people are more likely to encounter fairies at midsummer, especially Midsummer Eve (around June 21), the time of the summer solstice when the natural world is at its full peak. Other times are the first day of every quarter of the year, when fairies are said to pack up and move house.

Fairies Are Ghosts or Associated with the Dead

Fairies live underground, and thus have connections to the dead. Ghosts are really fairies, according to this view. Associations with the dead are particularly strong in the folklore of Brittany, France. The dead are summoned by the *ankou*, the King of the Dead, to join his invisible band. The Cherokee of North Carolina, who have a rich fairy lore, also associate fairies with their dead ancestors.

Fairies Are the Souls of the Pagan Dead

This is a Christianized version of the belief that fairies are ghosts. Only people who were not baptized Christian become fairies at death, and they are trapped between Heaven and Earth. This belief may have served to reinforce the importance of Christian baptism and to convert people from pagan beliefs to Christianity in order to avoid an unhappy fate.

Souls of the pagan dead are doomed to join bands of demonized pagan gods and goddesses, hellhounds, and witches. They participate in **wild hunts**, hordes of demonic figures that fly about at night, especially on the eve of Beltane (May 1), a Celtic fire and fertility festival.

One of the earliest written accounts of fairies in the British Isles comes from the witchcraft confession of Isobel Gowdie, a Scottish woman tried as a witch in 1662. Gowdie freely acknowledged consorting with fairies and gave vivid descriptions of the finely clothed King and Queen of Faery, their wonderful food, and their lively elf-bulls. The fairies and other witches were given magical arrowheads (called **elf-shot**), shaped by the devil with his own hand, she said. The witches shot them off their hands. Anything human or animal struck by elf-shot would immediately fall dead.

Gowdie was not the only witch to confess involvements with devilish fairies. However, because many witches were tortured until they confessed, some of their accounts may have been lies told to satisfy their inquisitors.

Fairies Are Fallen Angels

This is another Christianized explanation that reduces the importance of fairies by demonizing them. According to this view, fairies

Fairy Tales

Fairy tales are fictional stories with supernatural characters and elements, including fairies, witches, wizards, giants, monsters, dragons, talking animals, and other creatures. The term *fairy tale* has come to mean any far-fetched story. Though fictional, fairy tales are based on people's real experiences and many contain moral lessons. The descriptions of fairies in these stories are similar to those found in oral and written accounts of people's supposed real-life experiences with the Little Folk.

Fairy tales have been told since ancient times. One of the oldest and most famous collections is *Aesop's Fables*, stories collected by a Greek slave who lived from 620-560 BCE.

In the nineteenth century, authors, poets, and folklorists collected many of the oral fairy tales and published them in books. These collections are still in print today, entertaining people of all ages. In Germany, the brothers Jacob and Wilhelm Grimm collected stories now known as *Grimm's Fairy Tales.* The Danish author and poet Hans Christian Andersen collected stories as well. Scottish author Andrew Lang, who had a passionate interest in the paranormal, compiled stories into a series known as the "colored fairy books." Each book has a different color cover, such as red, blue, violet, yellow, and so on.

Pre-Islamic Arabian and Persian tales were translated into English by Sir Richard Burton and published as *The Book of 1001 Arabian Nights*. One of the best-known characters from these stories is the genie, a term derived from *djinn*. The djinn are like demons that act in ways similar to fairies. In the story "Aladdin's Wonderful Lamp," a genie is kept in an oil lamp. When the lamp is rubbed, the genie appears and is compelled to do the bidding of whoever holds the lamp. Aladdin uses the genie to become rich and powerful.

are angels who were cast out of heaven with Lucifer. Some of the fallen angels were too good to be sent to hell, so God condemned them to remain in the elements of the earth.

Different Origins, Common Ground

An interesting characteristic of fairy lore is that no matter where in the world they are found and regardless of their possible origins, descriptions of the Little People are strikingly similar when it comes to their appearances, shapes, clothing, activities, and temperament. In many cultures, they are thought to spend most of their time hidden from human eyes, they are considered tricksters and magical folk, and humans who encounter them are told to beware!

Meet the Fairies

On a pleasant summer evening in 1884, a postman drives his horse-drawn mail wagon around the Isle of Man, making his usual collections and deliveries. Residents of the Isle of Man, located in the Irish Sea between Ireland and England, are careful not to upset the fairies, which have a strong presence in the land. People on the island know that it is not wise to go looking for fairies, for trouble usually results. But every now and then an accidental encounter happens—and usually the human is on the losing side. So it goes that night for the unfortunate postman.

He is driving along, right on schedule, due at his destination with his bags at one o'clock in the morning, when his horse abruptly halts in the road. Swarming out from the roadside bushes comes a troop of little fairies, all smartly dressed in identical red suits and carrying little lanterns. With great glee, they jump aboard his wagon and heave the mail bags into the road, and then dance wildly in a circle around them. The postman, both terrified and annoyed, gets down and starts reloading the bags onto his wagon. But every time he replaces a bag, the fairies throw it back down on the road and keep dancing.

The postman struggles with the fairies for hours. He cannot shoo them away, and he cannot reload his wagon. The fairies pay no attention to him, save to thwart his attempts to put the mail bags back onto his wagon. They enjoy themselves immensely, dancing and jigging, and they show no signs of tiring.

Finally the first rays of dawn streak the sky. The light seems to signal to the fairies that their nighttime entertainment is at an end, and they disappear as suddenly as they appeared, vanishing into the brush. The exhausted postman collects his scattered bags and makes it to his destination at 5:30 in the morning without any more interference.

No one doubts his story. Everyone knows the mischief fairies make, without warning and for no apparent reason. The fairies never trouble the postman again on his route, but he gets nervous every time he reaches the place where the fairies attacked him.[1]

This account, related by the postman to a folklorist several years after the incident took place, describes a common encounter with fairies. They appear suddenly out of the natural world, little people usually ranging from 18 inches to 36 inches in height. They are either engaged in their own business or are dancing or singing. When they realize humans see them, they vanish. Sometimes they deliberately play tricks and create havoc with people, as they did with the Manx postman.

Accounts of fairies have been handed down orally over the centuries. Few were written down before the nineteenth century, which is not surprising. In earlier times not many people were educated to read and write. Stories were passed down among families and neighbors.

In the early years of the twentieth century, W.Y. Evans-Wentz, an American anthropologist, traveled throughout the British Isles and Brittany, France, to collect oral stories and accounts of fairies. His documentation (*The Fairy Faith in Celtic Countries*, 1911) preserves an invaluable record of Western fairy lore, drawn from the real experiences of people.

INVISIBLE PLAYMATES

It is not unusual for children to see and talk to playmates that adults cannot see. Adults often dismiss the playmates as the products of childish imaginations. However, children's descriptions of their appearances often match those found in fairy folklore. Fairies are fond of children and they love to play, sing, dance, and have a good time. Perhaps those visitors aren't imaginary but real little people.

Children are thought to be more psychically open than adults. Thus, it may be easier for them to perceive the little folk. Fairies, in turn, may choose to make themselves visible to certain people they like. They visit for a period of time, perhaps months or even a few years, and then leave, never to return again. They may leave because a child loses interest or moves away from a place that fairies frequent, or because adults have discouraged or forbidden children to tell stories of their invisible playmates.

In one case, children who claimed to have seen fairies were laughed at by their parents. The children decided to get revenge and created what came to be known as the Cottingley Fairy Hoax (see page 34).

DESCRIPTIONS OF FAIRIES

Fairies come in all shapes and sizes, but most accounts of them describe small versions of humans. They are smartly dressed, and their favorite colors are red and green. Often their skin is green, too. They love to wear little red caps. Usually they look youthful, but sometimes they appear wrinkled and wizened, as if very old. When seen—usually accidentally—they are out in nature, in the woods and gardens. Some of them like to come into households and live.

Not all fairies are small, however. In Irish and Scottish lore, the Sidhe are taller than humans, graceful and elegant in their bearing. They are organized in royal courts with kings and queens. There are two types of Sidhe, the **Seelie Court**, or Blessed Court, and the Unseelie (Unblessed) Court. Within both courts are numerous types of fairies.

The Seelie Court includes the good fairies, who are hardworking and industrious, and who live in a beautiful world of perpetual twilight. They do not seek out humans, but occasionally invite a deserving one into their realm. They seldom disturb humans unless disturbed

Figure 2.1 *A fairy digs in its garden, which is threatened by litter and encroaching construction.* (Fortean Picture Library)

themselves, for example, if they are insulted or their homes or travel ways are damaged.

The **Unseelie Court** is dark and dangerous, full of malevolent fairies who intensely dislike people. The Unseelie fairies are the dark opposites of the Seelie fairies. The Unseelies look for opportunities to harm people and their homes and animals, for they consider them to be enemies and a threat to their own world.

Among the Unseelies are the **Sluagh**, or "The Host," who come from the souls of the unsanctified dead, and monsters such as the nuckelavee. This Scottish sea creature is half horse and half human and rises up out of the sea to lay waste to the landscape, killing everything in its path.

Redcap is another famous member of the Unseelie Court. This goblin looks like " a short thickset old man, with long prominent teeth, skinny fingers armed with talons like eagles, large eyes of a fiery-red color, grisly hair streaming down his shoulders, iron boots, a pikestaff in his left hand, and a red cap on his head."[2] The cap is red because the evil fairy dips it in the blood of his victims.

HELPFUL FAIRIES

Some fairies, such as the **brownie**, are little people who come to live in homes, where they help keep things neat and clean. In return they expect offerings of food, especially milk, cream, honey, and sweets. In lore, any food that falls on the floor is claimed by the fairies and should not be eaten by human or animal. If no offerings are made or if humans insult the fairies by offering them money, the fairies become angry and make messes at night while the occupants of the home are asleep. They also will make messes if humans are not themselves neat and clean. Similar fairies help with farm chores, such as tending animals and planting and harvesting crops.

Another class of helpful fairies works in mines. They are called kobolds in German lore, knockers in Cornish lore, and tommyknockers in American lore. They toil away in mines, sounds of their work echoing like knocks through the mine shafts. They are said to knock warnings to miners to alert them to unsafe areas or impending collapses.

Garden and nature fairies tend to plants, trees, and flowers, helping them to grow and flourish. Some of these fairies are quite tiny, as described in the following accounts.

In 1977 Cynthia Montefiore was visiting her mother at her home in Somerset, England, where she had an unexpected sighting of a little winged fairy. Her mother offered to show Cynthia the proper way to cut a rose tree, and the two of them went out into the garden. Before any blooms could be snipped, the mother froze and pointed to one of the roses. According to Cynthia:

> With astonishment I saw what she was seeing—a little figure about six inches high, in the perfect shape of a woman and with brilliantly colored diaphanous wings

resembling those of a dragonfly. The figure held a little wand and was pointing it at the heart of the rose. At the tip of the wand there was a little light, like a star. The

The Great Fairy Hoax

Around the turn of the twentieth century, two girls in Cottingley, Yorkshire, England, loved to go out into the woods and play. They were joined by friendly playmates who were not of this world, but came from Fairyland. But when Elsie Wright and her cousin Frances Griffiths told their parents about the fairies, the adults laughed at them and told them it was only their imagination.

The girls, aged 17 and 9, determined to get even. In 1917, they took their camera into the woods, and soon they had five "fairy photos" to show. The images captured cute, little winged fairies in the woods. The photographs were black-and-white, because color photography did not exist at the time. The girls said the bodies of the fairies were white, and the wings were pale green, mauve, and pink.

The photos were actually fakes. The girls had cut out illustrations from magazines and photographed them against the woods and bushes. To their astonishment, serious adults believed the photographs to be real! Suddenly, Elsie and Frances were afraid to admit their prank.

The fairy photographs were sent around to experts. One of them was Sir Arthur Conan Doyle, the man who created the Sherlock Holmes mysteries. Doyle was a smart man, but he wanted—perhaps a bit too much—to believe in evidence proving the existence of spirits. He pronounced the photographs to be genuine.

Doyle wrote a book about the case, *The Coming of the Fairies*, published in 1922. In it, he said that more evidence proving fairies would be found. The girls became famous. After the book came out, Doyle left England for a long lecture tour in Australia. When he returned, he found he was being ridiculed all over the world. The Cottingley fairy photos had

figure's limbs were a very pale pink and visible through her clothes. She had long silvery hair which resembled an aura. She hovered near the rose for at least two minutes,

Figure 2.2 *"Fairies" float in the foreground of this hoax photograph created by two young girls in Cottingley, Yorkshire, England, in 1917.* (Fortean Picture Library)

been examined by more experts and were exposed as fakes. Doyle had to admit that he was the victim of a hoax.

Elsie and Frances remained quiet about their hoax until the 1980s, long after Doyle was dead. They finally admitted that they had faked the photos, but they insisted that they really had seen and played with fairies in the Cottingley woods.

her wings vibrating rapidly like those of a hummingbird, and then she disappeared.[3]

The women were so awe-struck that they returned to the house without cutting any roses.

Another experience of tiny winged fairies occurred in 1993. Karen Maralee was camping alone at Mt. Shasta in northern California, an area famous for sightings of fairies, aliens, Bigfoot, ghosts, and other mysterious creatures. One night at dusk, she suddenly heard what sounded like children singing. Karen followed the sounds and came upon a clearing where she saw 11 tiny blue fairies, about one foot tall, with bodies colored an electric blue that flickered and were semi-transparent. The beings had delicate, lacy wings that were larger than their bodies. The sight made Karen catch her breath. When she finally exhaled, the fairies heard her and disappeared. They left behind them 11 little piles of blue dust. Karen collected some of the dust, which she believed to have beneficial magical powers.[4]

Some nature fairies do not have human forms, but are described as shapes of light and color that live within the plant or tree that they serve. They have the ability to come out within a limited distance. When they do, they can shape-shift to a small human form. They come out at night and when they are interested in a human who appreciates the beauty of nature. They are constantly watching, which may be one reason why so many people feel watched in a forest, especially at twilight and night.[5]

MISCHIEVOUS FAIRIES

Fairies have a trickster nature, and some of them excel at playing pranks on humans. The tricks can be harmless but vexing, such as what happened to the Manx postman, or they can be deadly, such as when a traveler is led astray at night into a fatal accident.

In Cornish lore, which comes from Cornwall, a part of the British Isles, one of the dominant tricksters is the **pixie** or pishkey, originally a type of mine fairy. To be pixie-led means to be led astray or off course. In earlier times, travelers at night were in danger of being pixie-led by bouncing lights that took them into bogs, marshes, or lakes, where they drowned. Today "pixie-led" also refers to being led astray in thinking or decision-making.

LEPRECHAUNS

In Irish lore, **leprechauns** are solitary fairies. They do not go about in groups. They are dressed in green with a little green cap, and they smoke a long-stemmed golden pipe. They guard the pot of gold that lies at the end of the rainbow. According to lore, if one can look a leprechaun straight in the eye, it must take the person to the treasure. But if the person drops his or her gaze for even a second, the leprechaun will vanish—and so will the treasure.

DWARFS

Dwarfs come from German lore. "Dwarf" is actually an Old English term. Dwarf-like beings appear in many mythologies. They are small, stunted, and grotesque people who travel about in troops. Some are said to have great strength, and others are said to attend noble ladies in court. Some excel in thievery.

In the fairy tale *Snow White and the Seven Dwarfs*, benevolent dwarfs take pity on Snow White, who has fled her murderous stepmother, the queen, who is jealous of Snow White's beauty. The dwarfs agree to help Snow White and to grant whatever she wishes if she will keep house for them, cook, clean, and sew.

ELVES

Elves come from German and Scandinavian lore. Originally, they were believed to be a separate race of nature beings and gods. Most of them were beautiful and possessed great magical powers, including the ability to enchant humans. Some, however, were ugly. Elves lived in a hidden, magical world where time passed very slowly compared to human time. Some elves were as large as human in physical form.

Like fairies, elves enjoyed dancing in the moonlight. They intermingled with humans, and produced hybrid offspring in human-elf marriages. Some, such as gnomes, took up residence in human homes and helped with chores. But, like the fairy brownies, they could become nasty if displeased with human behavior.

Elves were absorbed into Celtic and European fairy lore, where they are divided into two classes, light and dark elves, similar to the Seelie

Celebrity Fairies and Elves

A handful of celebrity fairies and elves have shaped ideas about them over the centuries. Here's a who's who of famous fairies and elves.

Puck: Pucks are friendly but mischievous and given to pranks. Shakespeare gave one of his fairy characters in *A Midsummer Night's Dream* the proper name of Puck, and it stuck. Puck describes himself as "a merry wanderer of the night" who drinks and jokes with the elf king and queen, Oberon and Titania.

Robin Goodfellow: Another type of mischievous hobgoblin, an alter-ego to Puck. In earlier times, Robin G. and his fellow cloven-hoofed pucks were wicked and linked to the devil, but Shakespeare made them funny and popular.

Tom Thumb: A tiny lad in the lore of King Arthur who has many heroic adventures. Tomb Thumb is born by magic when a farmer and his wife who yearn for a son seek the help of the wizard Merlin. They want a son at any cost, even if he is no bigger than the farmer's thumb.

and Unseelie courts. The term *elf* was often used interchangeably with *fairy* and appeared in literature. Shakespeare featured Oberon and Titania, the king and queen of elves, in *A Midsummer Night's Dream*.

In the nineteenth century, Christmas became an increasingly popular festival. Scandinavian writers of fairy lore portrayed elves as the merry little helpers of Santa Claus in his annual chores of making and distributing gifts, and tending to his sleigh and elven reindeer. According to Christmas lore, the elves live with Santa in his secret village at the North Pole. They wear red and green clothing, slippers with pointed toes, and long caps.

Tinkerbell: In J.M. Barrie's play and novel *Peter and Wendy*, written at the turn of the twentieth century, Tinkerbell is a common fairy who repairs pots and kettles—a real tinker—and speaks in a voice like tinkling bells. She exists in Neverland, and befriends Peter Pan and his friend Wendy. For the movie *Peter Pan* (1953) Walt Disney turned her into a cute, little, winged thing scattering pixie dust everywhere, and she became an icon of fairies.

Elrond: In J.R.R. Tolkien's *Lord of the Rings*, Elrond is one of the wisest and most important elves in Middle-earth. Half-human and half-elf, he chose the elvish life and the right to immortality. After leading the fight against the evil power of the ring, Elrond chooses to sail the Western sea to Undying Lands, where he can rejoin his beloved wife and other immortal elves. The price is leaving behind his daughter, Arwen, who makes a different choice.

Arwen: Elrond's beautiful daughter, also called Undomiel, or "Evenstar." She sacrifices her right to sail west to the Undying Lands with her father, giving her place to the hobbit Frodo so that he might be healed of his wounds. She marries the human hero Aragorn, and spends 120 happy years with him.

It may seem that the huge task of assembling the world's Christmas presents would require an army of elves working night and day all year long, but according to lore, there are only a handful of them, between 6 and 13, according to different accounts.

The British author J.R.R. Tolkien probably did the most to popularize elves in his trilogy *Lord of the Rings*, about the heroic adventures of hobbits and elves against the forces of evil, centered on a fight to control an all-powerful magical ring. Whoever owns the ring commands absolute, total power.

The hobbits and elves live in Middle-earth, a place comparable to Fairyland. The hobbits are little people, about half the size of the average human. They have unusually big feet.

The hero hobbit, Bilbo Baggins, and his fellow hobbits are aided by the wizard Gandalf and join forces with the elves of Rivendell under the leadership of their lord, Elrond. Their adventures take them into mines abandoned by dwarfs, and they do battle with orcs, monstrous and evil descendants of elves. Ultimately, the forces of good win. But Bilbo is forever changed, and he sails off to the Undying Lands, the immortal abode of the elves.

Where Fairies Live

Thomas the Rhymer is a respected Scottish laird and poet in the thirteenth century. He lives at Ercildoune, later to be known as Earlston. Unexpectedly, he gains the powers of prophecy, a gift from the Queen of Elfland, who becomes infatuated with him.

Thinking him a handsome and desirable man, the queen kidnaps Thomas and spirits him to Elfame, also called Elfland or the land of the fairies, a place few mortals are ever privileged to see. It is a beautiful place of eternal light, pleasure, and happiness. Thomas enjoys himself there for seven earthly years.

At the end of that time, the fairies face a reckoning. Every seven years, they must pay a *teind*, or tithe, to the devil. The tithe is a fairy chosen by the devil himself. The fairies worry that the devil will choose fair Thomas.

The queen reluctantly sends Thomas back to the mortal world, bestowing on him the gift of a tongue that cannot lie. Thomas returns to his life in Ercildoune and becomes famous as a prophet of great accuracy.

As years go by the queen cannot let go of her love for him. One night, while Thomas eats a feast in his castle, a man runs in to warn that a hind and doe have left the forest, heading for the castle. Knowing the deer to be fairies in disguise, Thomas goes out to greet them. He follows them into the forest and is never seen again.

According to lore, Thomas returned to Elfland, where he continues to serve as a counselor to the fairies. Every now and then, mortals who visit Elfame catch a glimpse of him, eternally young and happy.[1]

The story of Thomas the Rhymer is told in the "Ballad of True Thomas," which circulated in various versions through the sixteenth to nineteenth centuries. The story is based on a fourteenth-century romance fairy tale, perhaps told to explain the sudden onset of Thomas's prophetic powers. Other mortals who claimed to visit the land of fairies have told similar stories through the ages of a wondrous place where time passes very slowly.

Most fairies live beneath the ground in a secret land. The doorway to their land is a mound or fort, also called a **howe** or **knowe** in Scotland, and a **rath** in Ireland. The doorway is usually closed to mortals, but occasionally a person accidentally stumbles through. Sometimes the fairies kidnap humans they like and bring them to their land.

A HEALING GIFT FOR KIDNAPPED ANNE JEFFRIES

Like Thomas the Rhymer, Anne Jeffries was a human who caught the fancy of fairies. She lived in St. Teath, Cornwall, England, in the seventeenth century. Anne was a bright and intelligent girl, and she was fascinated by fairies. At dusk, a favored time to see fairies, she would go out into the countryside and turn over fern leaves, singing rhymes to invite the fairies to show themselves.

At age 19 she was hired as a servant girl to the Pitt family, and she looked after their young son, Moses. In 1645 she fell into a mysterious fit and was sick for a long time. When she recovered, she said that she had been taken away by the fairies. Now she had the gift of healing by touch, and she was clairvoyant as well, that is, she could see the invisible spirits and realms.

According to Anne, she was knitting one day outside the garden when she heard a rustling. At first, she thought it was her sweetheart

Figure 3.1   *Fairies live in a secret underground world that is usually inaccessible to humans.* (Mary Evans Picture Library/Arthur Rackman/The Image Works)

coming to see her. Instead, six little men entered the arbor. They were handsome with bright, shiny eyes, and were dressed in green. The leader had a red feather in his cap. He spoke in a loving voice to her and climbed up on her lap, kissing her on the neck. The others climbed up and began kissing her, too. One put his hands over her eyes, and Anne suddenly found herself whisked through the air. When she opened her eyes, she found she was in Fairyland.

A beautiful landscape stretched before her. There were temples and palaces of gold and silver, lakes filled with gold and silver fish, wondrous trees, brilliant flowers, and brightly colored birds that sang sweetly. Anne's clothing had changed, and she was now dressed as finely as the fairies. Strangely, they were no longer little, but the size of humans.

Anne continued to be romanced by the leader of her band of admirers. She was supremely happy and decided she could stay in Fairyland forever. But jealousy erupted among the fairy men, who fought with her lover, wounding him in a sword fight. Once again Anne's eyes were covered, and she was sent sailing through the air with a great humming noise. When she opened them again, she found herself back at the Pitt home.

Anne was never able to visit Fairyland again, but the fairies continued to visit her. They gave her fairy food, which sustained her in good health, and she was seldom seen to eat the food of mortals. People flocked to her for healing and prophecy.

At the time, fairies were often associated with witchcraft and the devil. Fear of witches was high. Anne was arrested on charges of witchcraft and imprisoned and was not given food to eat. Her health remained good, and she never complained, for the fairies fed her.

Eventually Anne was released. She became a servant of a widowed aunt of Moses Pitt. She married a laborer, William Warren.

Moses Pitt tried to get Anne to tell her story about the fairies for publication, but she refused. Stung and perhaps bitter by the foul treatment she had received, she said she did not want her name spread all over in books and ballads.[2]

Fairyland: You Can Check In But You Can't Check Out

According to the lore of fairies, it is forbidden for human beings to enter their realm uninvited. Someone who stumbles accidentally into Fairyland may be held prisoner for a very long time, perhaps even forever. The only way to exit is if the fairies decide to cast out the intruder. But it could be pleasant, despite the fact that the person would never see the human world again.

Good fairies don't put people in jail. Instead, they prevent them from leaving by feeding them enchanted food or by using magical spells to bewitch them into a state of happy drowsiness. Since the passage of time is slow in Fairyland, visitors don't realize how long they stay there. The food is delicious and the place is beautiful, so imprisoned humans may not mind never going home to the Land Above.

Reverend Robert Kirk was familiar with the folk wisdom warning against eating fairy food. Even though he was invited to visit Fairyland, he avoided fairy food, which smelled and looked irresistible. His mouth watered over and over again at the sight and scent of fairy feasts. Finally, his fairy host urged him to sample the food. He cautiously took a piece of bread and tasted what he said was "the finest loaf ever created." He followed that with a sip of water that was bright, clear, and pure. His fairy host told him that only people of good heart could taste fairy food. All others would taste dust and ashes. Kirk concluded that the food itself did not have magical properties that imprisoned people in Fairyland, but that the pleasure of eating it was so great people would not want to leave and give it up.

Bad fairies who do not like people are not so generous. If a person enters their world without permission, they say they have the right to take his or her life.

Some say that Anne's trip to Fairyland was nothing more than delusion, perhaps brought on in a delirium during her illness. According to fairy lore, her illness was caused by her kidnapping, and the spiriting away of her true self to an enchanted land.

ROBERT KIRK'S ADVENTURES IN FAIRYLAND

The most famous traveler to Fairyland was Reverend Robert Kirk of Aberfoyle, Scotland, a place steeped in fairy lore. Kirk was fascinated by it and loved to spend time around the fairy howes.

On the night of the full moon in May 1692, Kirk took a trip that few mortals have experienced and lived to tell about. Kirk was wandering about a known fairy howe, or mound, that night, drinking in the beauty of the darkness lit by the pearly lunar glow. Suddenly he heard a strange and inviting music, unlike anything played by humans. A bright light then shone from within the mound, as though a doorway had opened.

Lured by the music and the light, Kirk went closer and found he could see straight into the mound. A stone passage led downward into the depths of the mound, and the bright light shone from an unknown end. A wondrous scent like roses drifted up the passageway.

Kirk felt pulled into the passageway but hesitated because he recalled the warnings of his father, that the wee folk were hostile to people and wicked in their ways. Then he remembered also stories of good fairies told by his kin and neighbors. At last his curiosity got the better of him, and he descended down the passage toward the light, the music, and the intoxicating scent of roses.

He walked and walked, much farther than the length of the howe, going down and down. He later wrote in his diary, "Then suddenly, as I was mindful of turning back, I emerged into a place of such wonder that even now I am scarcely able to describe it without trembling."[3]

Kirk beheld a cavern so big that the entire city of Aberfoyle and much of the land around it could have fit inside. The walls glowed with light. Hundreds of elegant and exotic beings, such as he had never seen before, were dancing. Some were taller than any living person, very noble, bright, and stately. Others were smaller and seemed dressed in clothing made of tree bark or animals skins.

Kirk gazed speechlessly upon this scene, and then he was bidden to dance with the fairies. He did, though he felt clumsy in the face of their grace. He was approached by two regal beings, the King and Queen of Fairyland. They spoke in musical voices and told him he was welcome in their land. They knew he had spent much time studying their ways, and they thought it fitting that he should see firsthand how fairies lived. Most people who entered Fairyland were never allowed to leave, but Kirk would be allowed to return home to his family, they said.

In the weeks that followed, Kirk made trips to the howe and knocked upon it to gain his secret entry, as he had been taught. He met different kinds of fairies, saw them at work and play, and got answers to his questions about them. He was almost always accompanied by a guide named Kee, who provided information that had been passed down orally for thousands of years. Once Kirk was allowed into a huge library, but the books were written in a language he could not understand.

Kee explained that fairies came from the earth just as humans had in the beginning, but they had arrived on earth much earlier. They lived simple lives in wild places. Then humans—who the fairies called the Newcomers—arrived and began to hunt down fairies and kill them. The fairies moved into more remote areas and finally retreated into the earth.

Kirk was impressed with the elegance, industriousness, and beauty of many of the fairies. Their entire world and everything in it was always lit by a pleasant inner glow.

Once Kirk decided to take an action forbidden to him. He ventured into the dark kingdom of the Unseelie Court, where evil fairies lived. He hoped to prevent the Seelie and Unseelie courts from warring against each other. Kirk found himself in a dim world lit by the moon and cast in thick shadows. He had an audience with the king and queen, who were the exact, dark opposites of the king and queen of the Seelie Court.

The rulers angrily informed Kirk that he had trespassed into their realm, and they had legal rights to have him executed as punishment. Kee intervened, and Kirk was taken before the king and queen of the Seelie Court. They told him that he could choose death or permanent exile to the land of the good fairies. He would be allowed one last visit to his family to set his affairs in order. Kirk chose exile. He left his diary of his fairy adventures for his family, with a final date of June 21, 1692.

According to historical records, Kirk went out in his nightshirt on the evening of June 21 and went to his favorite fairy howe. He collapsed. Later he was found and carried home. A doctor pronounced him dead that night. He was 48 years old. The cause of his death may have been a heart attack or a stroke. Or, perhaps as he recorded in his diary, he died to the world of mortals and went to live among the fairies.

According to lore, Kirk appeared to a cousin after his death and delivered a message. He said that he was being held captive in Fairyland, but there was a way that he could be freed. Kirk's wife was pregnant at the time of his death. When the child was delivered, Kirk would appear as a ghost at his christening. The cousin was to throw an iron knife over Kirk's ghost. Iron, believed to weaken the power of fairies, would break the spell and enable Kirk to return to the land of mortals.

Kirk appeared at the christening, but the cousin lost his nerve and did not throw the knife. Kirk's ghost vanished, another captive of the fairies never to be seen again.

Kirk's diary of his fairy adventures was published after his death as *The Secret Commonwealth*. It is still in print today, and stands as one of the most detailed and remarkable descriptions of fairies and their lives and world.

The Life of Fairies

Long, long ago in Wales, a 10-year-old boy is miserable. He has trouble learning his lessons at school, and so the schoolmaster punishes him with whipping and cruel treatment. One day the boy cannot stand anymore, and he runs away from school. He sits by a riverbank, crying.

Soon some wee folk appear. They are the *Tylwyth Teg*, as fairies are called in Wales. They ask the boy why he is crying. He tells them, and the fairies reply that if he comes with them, he will not need to go to school for as long as he likes.

The boy agrees, and the fairies whisk him away under the water and over the water into an underground cave that opens into a great palace. There the boy sees fairies dancing and singing in rings and playing games with golden balls. This is the fairy king's family and court. The boy joins in the games and is given a golden ball. For the first time in a long time, he is happy.

Soon the boy tires of the games and misses his own home and family. He takes his ball and retraces his route through the cave to the river. At the riverside, two fairies stop him, take away his ball, and push him into the water. He finds his way home, where he apologizes to his mother for being gone for two weeks. His shocked mother tells him he has been gone for two years, and she had given up on him as dead.

The boy tries to find the entrance to the land of the *Tylwyth Teg* again, but it is lost to him forever. He goes back to school and becomes an excellent student.[1]

The story above is part of Welsh fairy lore. It is told in different versions in lore elsewhere. The boy is probably fictional, but the story itself is based on the real experiences of people who are given a glimpse of life in Fairyland. The fairies are choosy about their guests and usually offer their hospitality only once.

ENCHANTED LIVES

Fairies occupy themselves much as humans do, working at jobs and entertaining themselves with song and dance. They have communities, get married, and have children. They have longer life spans than mortals; in some lore, they are immortal.

Fairies are always in a good mood when left alone, but they can become irritated and angry when humans interfere with them or even see them accidentally. Left to themselves, they are happy no matter what they do. Though their activities are similar to those of humans, they do not suffer illness or misfortune.

Fairies are famous for their skill in industry and crafts, and they go about their jobs with great enthusiasm, sometimes singing while they work. They are excellent metal workers, jewelry makers, weavers, farmers, herdsmen, miners, and bakers. They hold markets and fairs for their wares.

Nature spirit fairies tend things in nature, helping plants and crops to grow. They try to prevent humans from damaging or destroying their favorite things. They especially guard elder, oak, ash, blackthorn, and hazel trees.

A story is told about a cottager in Ireland who tried to cut a branch of a sacred elder tree that was hanging over a sacred well. This angered the fairies who looked after the tree. Twice they stopped the man by sending him an alarm that his house was burning. He went racing

Figure 4.1 *Fairies weave curtains from leaves in an underground room. Fairies are known for their skill in industry and craftsmanship.* (Mary Evans Picture Library/Arthur Rackman/The Image Works)

home, only to find the alarms were false. On the third try, he succeeded in cutting the branch. When he arrived home, he found his cottage burned to the ground. The fairies had their revenge![2]

A similar story concerns Heart Lake near Sligo, Ireland. The lake has long been said to be a passageway used by fairies to travel from their land to the mortal world. When a group of men tried to drain the lake, they were diverted by visions of their houses burning down. They rushed home, only to find that the visions were tricks played by the fairies.[3]

Another story tells of the consequences of cutting down two fairy thorns to clear land for a hospital in Kiltimagh, Ireland, around 1920. All the locals knew the fairy thorns were haunted by fairies and would not touch the trees out of fear of suffering the wrath of the little ones. Finally a man from out of town undertook the task and cut down the trees. When local lads warned him of the consequences, he angrily retorted, "I'll be back, never fear, and to hell with your bloody fairies!" That was a serious mistake, for one should never insult the fairies. That night the man suffered a stroke and was crippled. He died within a year. He did return to the town as he predicted but in a coffin. As for the hospital, it was built, but it never opened.[4]

Household fairies live in the homes of people they like and help with chores and tidying. Brownies and other home-based fairies demand neatness, cleanliness, and order. Some will not even consider going to a home that is unkempt and disorderly. They work to maintain order, and so they do not like humans to constantly undo their efforts.

Household fairies like to be rewarded for their work, but they are insulted if people try to pay them with money. In response, they will create messes or depart altogether. Instead of money, they appreciate offerings of food, milk, cream, and honey. They do not eat the actual food, but they take the essence of it. Eating food intended for fairies will make people and animals sick, according to lore.

If people leave no offerings, the fairies will depart in anger, sometimes leveling a curse upon the family or the land.

FAIRY ANIMALS

Like humans, fairies have animals. They tend fairy livestock, and they keep fairy dogs and cats as pets. Fairy animals are usually invisible, but sometimes they find their way into the human world.

A Welsh fairy tale tells about a farm wife who found a fairy dog lying exhausted on the ground. She picked it up, carried it home, and nursed it back to health. She did so not only out of the goodness of her heart but out of fear of the fairies. The woman's cousin had once found a fairy dog and had taken it home and treated it cruelly. When the fairies found out, they sent her on a harrowing flight through the air. She was dipped into bogs and swamps and tossed through briars, until all of her clothes were torn off and she was scratched and bleeding.

In due time the fairies found out where their dog was being kept and came to the farm wife to fetch it. They were pleased with her kindness and asked her if she would like the favor of a clean cow yard or a dirty cow yard. Knowing that a cow yard can be clean only if there are few cows in it, the farm wife said she would prefer a dirty cow yard. When the fairies departed, she found that she had been given two cows for every one she had. Their milk made the best butter ever tasted.[5]

Moral of this story? It pays to be nice to fairies!

FAIRY DANCES AND RINGS

Fairies love to dance, and their favorite dance is done in a circle on moonlit nights. Humans have come upon fairies, dressed up in bright red fancy clothes or uniforms, dancing away the night. They bounce round and round to sweet music played on fiddles and pipes, until the break of dawn. Sometimes they are joined by witches.

If the fairies notice humans watching them, they may draw them into their circle by enchantment. The humans then become prisoners, unable to leave the dance. A night of dancing in fairy time can equal years in human time. The human prisoners can escape only if they are pulled out by other humans or if the fairies end their dance and leave the humans unconscious on the ground.

Sometimes fairies react in anger and punish humans who observe them, for they do not like to be seen. On the Isle of Man a story is told about a man named William Nelson, who was out fishing late one night. On his way home he spied a large group of fairies in red coats dancing in a pea field. As he watched in wonder an old woman fairy came up to him and spat in his eyes, declaring, "You'll never see us again." Nelson was blinded for the rest of his life.[6]

When fairies leave their dance, a ring remains on the ground, marked by a circle of mushrooms. The mushrooms are inedible. The mushrooms grow naturally in rings, but their association with fairies has lent them magical properties, according to lore. For example, if someone stands in the middle of a fairy ring on the night of the full moon and makes a wish, the wish will come true. To see fairies, run around a fairy ring nine times on the night of a full moon.

FAIRY RADES

Another favored fairy activity is the *rade*, or ride, a procession of fairies on horseback. The fairy rade takes fairies into the land of mortals. The most important rades occur on Midsummer Night's Eve, the summer solstice, which occurs June 21 or 22. Midsummer Night's Eve is the peak of summer and the time when fairies undertake their biggest celebrations and entertainment. They wear their finest clothing and dress their fairy horses in jewels. In earlier times people often stayed indoors on this night, fearing that if they saw fairies, bad luck would follow. The most dangerous night of all was Samhain, now known as Halloween, the night when the dead have free reign over the earth. They join with fairies in their rades and roam about playing havoc with the living.

Reverend Robert Kirk said he was taken along on a celestial rade. The procession began, and the horses raced faster and faster, until the landscape became a blur. Kirk hung on for dear life. He was terrified to see that his horse and the entire procession had left the earth and were flying through the air. He said,

> What a magnificent sight I beheld! The Faery Rade spread out across the sky like a trail of stars, or a fiery comet's tail. Around us the vast expanse of the heavens glowed and glittered, lit by the great round face of the Midsummer moon.[7]

The fairies sang as they rode. Kirk did not know how much time passed, but at some point he was returned to the entrance of the fairy howe and was told that the rest of the night was for fairies alone.

FAIRY SPORTS AND GAMES

Fairies love to hunt for sport. On the Isle of Man they have been seen astride their horses, dressed in green, and blowing their huntsmen horns as they fly swiftly about the land in pursuit of fairy game.

Fairies also like to play chess, a game of skill for warfare and ruling, and hurling, an ancient Gaelic game played with a ball and sticks similar to field hockey. Sometimes fairies play hurling in competition with mortals.[8]

GUARDING TREASURES

Leprechauns are shoemakers in Irish lore. They also are specially charged with guarding hordes of treasure and pots of gold and money. Leprechauns are different from many other fairies. They are usually alone, instead of in groups. They wear green clothes and cap, and they smoke a long-handled pipe. They are not as good-looking as other fairies.

Leprechauns can lead a person to a pot of gold that rests at the end of the rainbow. The person must never take his or her eyes off the leprechaun, not even for a second, or he will vanish.

In other lore, if a leprechaun is captured, he must take a person to a hidden stash of gold or money. Catching a leprechaun is a difficult task, for they vanish easily in order to avoid capture.

Leprechauns may reveal the location of hidden treasure to a mortal, but when the person finds it and takes it home, it turns into something worthless, like a pile of dirt and leaves. Also, if a person knows about a secret treasure and reveals it to another person, the treasure becomes worthless or vanishes altogether.[9]

DO FAIRIES CHANGE WITH THE TIMES?

Most of the lore about fairies comes from earlier centuries, when people lived in small towns and villages. They farmed, owned livestock,

Figure 4.2 *A leprechaun takes a break from guarding his pot of gold and mends a pair of shoes.* (Fortean Picture Library)

and had simple lives. They saw fairies involved in activities that mirrored their own.

Do fairies today have televisions, computers, cell phones, automobiles, and other modern conveniences? There is evidence that they do.

In 1929 two children in Hertford, England, saw a tiny man piloting a tiny plane about the sky. The girl, five, and her brother, eight, were in their garden playing when they saw what looked like a toy biplane fly low over the fence. The wings were no more than 15 inches in length. The plane landed for a few minutes and then soared off, and the little pilot waved gaily to the children as he left. The children said he wore a leather flying helmet.[10]

In September 1979 four children between the ages of eight and 10 were playing in Wollaton Park in Nottingham, England. They all saw about 60 little men with long beards and wrinkled faces, wearing long caps and blue and yellow tights, who were racing about in little cars. There were two men to a car. The vehicles made no sounds and had the capability of leaping up into the air in order to clear obstacles. The fairies chased the children in their cars, laughing as though they were playing a game. The experience lasted for about 15 minutes.[11]

In modern times, fairies have been compared to extraterrestrial visitors who arrive in spaceships, a notion that will be explored in a later chapter.

Don't Mess with Fairy Tracks

Fairies have their own roads and highways like humans do. The problem for humans is that these roads are invisible. Misery comes to the person who builds a house on top of a fairy track or damages or destroys it. It doesn't matter to the fairies that the person didn't see it. They'll be mad, anyway. Their revenge: raining bad luck and disaster down upon the unlucky human.

If a house is built on a fairy track, the occupants will suffer mysterious illnesses. Their animals will sicken and die, and they will have nothing but misfortune. The houses will always be in disrepair and will even collapse. People who realize they are on top of a fairy track can improve their situation by keeping their doors or windows open at night so that the fairies can pass through.

How can humans know where these invisible fairy tracks are? One way is to consult the fairies before any construction is undertaken. Turn a piece of sod over, and check it the next day. If it has been left alone, the fairies have given permission for construction. But if the sod has been turned back over, the fairies disapprove, and wise humans will choose another site.[12]

Fairy Powers

A midwife who once lived in the village of Walchwyl, Switzerland, is summoned one night by a dwarf for her services. In the days before hospitals, women gave birth to their babies at home, usually assisted by skilled women called midwives.

The Swiss midwife is taken by the dwarf to a passageway in a rock, which opens into a magnificent hall. There the queen of the dwarfs is about to give birth. The midwife helps her bring a prince into the world.

The midwife is led out and shown the way home. In payment for her services, the dwarf guide presses something into her apron. He warns her not to look at it until she is inside her house. Bursting with curiosity, she cannot contain herself. As soon as the dwarf vanishes, she peeks. Her apron is filled with coals!

Enraged at this poor payment, she flings all but two of the coals on the ground. She takes the remaining two home to show her husband. When she arrives she throws them on the ground in disgust.

Her husband exclaims that they are not coals but precious jewels. The midwife still sees only coals. She consults a neighbor, who assures her that dwarfs disguise their gems as coals. But when the midwife runs back to where she had shaken out the coals, she finds they have all disappeared.[1]

GOOD LUCK, BAD LUCK

The story has many variations involving all kinds of fairies, including dwarfs, elves, and **trolls**. The tale illustrates the fairies' magical powers of bestowing great fortune and abundance upon humans in gratitude for work or a favor. The magic always is conditional, and if a taboo is broken—such as not peeking or rejecting the gift—the gift is taken back.

Though fairies like to be left alone most of the time, they ask humans for help every now and then. They are fond of borrowing tools and household items. The objects mysteriously disappear for a while, and then mysteriously reappear, usually with a payment of some sort, such as riches. It is not wise to get mad at the fairies or refuse their requests, for the fairies may cast bad luck spells.

A farmer in Strathspey, Scotland, was out sowing his field one day when a beautiful fairy woman appeared, carrying a poke, or sack. She asked him to sing her a song, and he obliged. Then she asked him to fill her poke with some of his seed. He obliged this, too. The fairy told him he would not miss any of the seed he had given her and then went on her way.

The farmer finished sowing his field and discovered, to his delight, that his seed sack was still full. He sowed several more fields, and the bag never emptied. Delighted at his good fortune, he returned home. His wife, spying the full sack, accused him of doing nothing all day, or taking seeds from a neighbor. At once the seed bag became empty, never to be endlessly filled again. The farmer's wife had broken another fairy taboo, to never question a gift from the fairies.[2]

Similarly, fairies do not like their own favors to humans to go unappreciated. If that happens, they take back whatever they have given and then some.

A story related in nineteenth-century Scottish lore concerns a sheep farmer, David Wright. The fairies aided him by cutting the grass in his meadow and piling it neatly in stacks for hay. In return for the labor, Wright always gave the fairies some of the best fleeces sheared from his sheep. Wright was always prosperous.

When he died, the farm was taken over by his greedy son. Young Wright decided the fairies should have none of his fleeces and ordered his servants to cut the hay instead of letting the fairies do it. The servants did as ordered, but every day their hay was scattered all over the meadow, until it rotted and was useless.

In revenge young Wright destroyed the fairy mounds and rings. But the fairies had the last lick. They stole his butter—a valued commodity back then—and made all his livestock sicken and die. One night when young Wright was returning home from market, the fairies led him astray, another of their powers. He fell into a well and died. The fairies' revenge did not end there. The Wright farmhouse fell into ruin and was torn down.[3]

One of the ways that fairies bring about misfortune is through elf-shot, tiny, poisonous arrows that kill whatever they pierce. Another way is to steal the essence out of food, which becomes worthless and even dangerous to eat.

Remedies against bad luck spells cast by fairies include prayers and signs of the cross to ward off the negative influences. Prayers must be said daily over livestock and the home, for example. A tradition exists to carve crosses in buns and loaves of bread, which blesses them and prevents the fairies from stealing their nutritional essence.

Travelers out at night turned their jackets and coats inside out in order to ward off being led astray. The inside-out coat is a common remedy in folklore against all kinds of troublesome spirits. It was believed that the turned coat would fool or confuse the spirits.

GLAMOUR AND INVISIBILITY

Not all fairies share the same powers. Another common power is **glamour**, that is, the ability to enchant someone to see something that is not real. Ugly fairies can make themselves look beautiful. Others can mislead travelers by showing them paths that actually lead to dangerous, even fatal places. Fairies play tricks by making worthless objects such as dirt, leaves, and stones look like treasures.

The biggest glamour is making themselves and their world invisible. If a person breaks the veil of the glamour accidentally, the fairies disappear. Or, if the fairies are angry, they strike the person in the eyes, blinding him.

The Reverend Robert Kirk learned one of the secrets of invisibility during his time in Fairyland. On Midsummer Eve fairies gather the seeds of a certain fern and use them to make themselves invisible. When the seeds are placed on the back of the hand, the fairies fade from view. The Reverend Robert Kirk tried this and found that when he placed seeds on the back of his hand, his entire body tingled and then became invisible.[1]

Some fairies make themselves invisible by wearing a magical cap, usually red in color. Other fairies have a magical ointment that, when rubbed on the eyes, enables a person to penetrate their glamour and see things for what they really are. The invisible becomes visible. Fairies may punish humans for using their ointment by blinding them.

LEVITATION

Fairies have the magical ability to levitate themselves and fly through the air but rarely with wings, which were inventions of artists and authors. Instead, fairies use magical caps, magical words, and traveling tools such as twigs, stems, and bundles of grasses. They levitate their horses. "Horse and Hattock" are two magical passwords recorded in lore. The seventeenth-century Scottish witch, Isobel Gowdie, who said she worked with fairies, revealed to inquisitors that her secret words for flying on cornstalks and rushes were "Horse and Hattock, in the Devil's name!"[5]

When fairies escort or kidnap mortals, they levitate them through the air. Levitation and flying also are used as punishment. The offending person is tossed about in rough winds and banged into trees and bushes.

Figure 5.1 *Two fairies fly past a group of birds. Fairies are also believed to possess powers of enchantment, invisibility, and healing, among other magical abilities.* (Mary Evans Picture Library/Arthur Rackman/The Image Works)

HEALING AND "THE SIGHT"

Two of the most important gifts that fairies give to humans are the ability to heal by touch and clairvoyance, or "the **Sight**," the ability to see the unseen and also the future. For example, Thomas the Rhymer was given both gifts by the Queen of Elfland.

In Wales the little lakeside village of Myddfai is reputed to be the home of famous healers who were taught their art by a water fairy, the Lady of the Lake. The lake is Llyn y Fan Fach (pronounced *chlinnuh van vach*). It is located in the Black Mountains, a wild, remote and spectacularly beautiful area.

The story goes that a young man is at the lake one day when a beautiful water fairy maiden rises up out of its waters. Smitten, he desires to marry her. Her father consents and gives her a fine dowry

Iron: Fairy Kryptonite

Want to make fairies weaken and flee? Get a piece of iron. According to lore, iron saps their strength and repels them. Why is iron so effective? Various explanations are given in lore, but the bottom line is not even the fairies know for certain.

Since ancient times iron has been regarded as having magical strengths and properties. Perhaps early humans believed this because human blood contains iron and has an iron smell. Iron weapons and tools thus held the magic of the life force and could protect people against evil spirits, witches, and fairies.

Reverend Robert Kirk asked his fairy friends about iron, and was told that to the best of their knowledge, fairies had no protection against the iron swords of early humans when fairies still lived above ground. The metal burned them. The worst effect was caused by cold iron, that is, pure iron not smelted from ore and hammered without melting.

To protect against fairy kidnappings, especially of newborns, people once placed iron scissors beneath pillows or hung them over beds. Iron nails and iron horseshoes driven into walls and over doorways prevented fairies from entering a house or stable. An old English custom in the game of croquet called for pounding an iron nail into the balls and mallets to prevent fairy tricks.

Curiously, other fairy lore contradicts the weakening power of iron. Kirk reported that fairies eventually learned how to make their own weapons and tools from iron, although they preferred gold and bronze. In Celtic lore, the kobolds are the fairy smiths, artfully working metals of all sorts without any ill effects. Ironworking fairies also are found in Asian lore.

of cattle. He places one condition upon his son-in-law: that he never strike his daughter or touch her with iron. If he does so three times, she will return to the lake forever.

The two marry and have four sons. They are very happy, but over the course of time the husband forgets himself and strikes his wife. He does not give her blows but taps her. The first time, he gives her a light tap to hurry her along when she is late. The second time, he tries to stop her from crying at a wedding. The third time, he tries to stop her from laughing at a funeral.

Upon the third tap, she takes all of her cattle and they all disappear forever back into the lake. But before she goes, she teaches her fairy arts of healing to her sons. They become the sires of a long line of respected physicians. Myddfai becomes known for its physicians and also for its fair maidens.[6]

The story illustrates several beliefs about fairies:

1 They have magical powers and gifts to bestow.

2 They marry mortals but always with conditions.

3 If the conditions are broken, they vanish and take back everything they brought with them.

FAIRY GODMOTHERS

Fairies are renowned for their fondness for children, including human ones. A **fairy godmother** is a special female fairy that watches over human children and bestows blessings upon the household in a role similar to that of a guardian angel.

The origins of the fairy godmother are found in pagan fairy lore that tells of fairies visiting homes when a newborn child is named. This lore, like other parts of fairy lore, became Christianized over time. Romantic ballads and stories featured fairy godmothers that attended Christian baptisms. They guarded the young children, sometimes bestowing some of their magical gifts and abilities on them.

6

Bad Fairies

One dark night in Norway, a farm boy hurries home. He is late and had not intended to be out after the sun went down. It is not vampires or ghosts that worry him but the dreaded **Sea Draugs**, fairies that are the souls of unbaptized men who died at sea. Hideous and wicked, they fly through the air at night, looking for mortal prey.

The boy tries to be quiet and invisible, but soon he hears a horrible noise, growing louder. It is the screeching Sea Draugs, scouring the landscape, looking for people to snatch up and carry off. The boy runs in terror.

The Sea Draugs catch sight of him and chase. They are fast and have the advantage of flying. They will catch him before he gets home.

Quick thinking saves the boy. He races to the Christian cemetery of the village, calling out to the souls of the sanctified dead to protect him. They rise up and fend off the angry fairies. The boy makes it safely back to his farm.

The Sea Draugs have the last word. In revenge, they trash the cemetery, overturning and breaking headstones. The destruction is testimony to the truth of the boy's story.[1]

The Sea Draugs are similar to other bad fairies in lore. Most fairies are benign, even benevolent, provided humans respect them and mind their manners. Good fairies will play tricks and punish wrongdoing humans, but most of them will not go out of their way to make trouble.

Every society has its villains, however, even the fairies. Bad fairies dislike people and animals and commit evil deeds against them.

THE WILD HUNT

Today, October 31, Halloween, is one of the most dreaded nights of the year, when spirits and tricksters are said to have free reign to play havoc. In earlier times the night of April 30 rivaled or even exceeded October 31 as the scariest of times. It was the night of the Wild Hunt.

May 1 was one of the biggest agrarian festivals, celebrating fertility, the coming of summer, and the growing of crops and vegetation. Known in Celtic lore as Beltane, the festival has ancient, pagan roots. As Christianity spread, the festival was given darker and demonic associations. The eve of the festival, called Beltane Eve or *Walpurgisnacht*, belonged to the spirits, especially the unholy. Walpurgisnacht is a German term meaning "night of Walburga."[2] St. Walburga was a popular saint, an Englishwoman who founded a convent in Germany in the eighth century. Because her feast day falls on May 1, her name has become associated with the celebration.

On Walpurgisnacht the Wild Hunt terrorized the skies. It was a group of witches, demons, pagan gods and goddesses, fairies, and the unbaptized dead. They rode astride their black, red-eyed demon horses, accompanied by their howling, yowling hellhounds and phantom black dogs. The Wild Hunt soared through the air, shrieking and making hideous noises. They punished the lazy and hunted the souls of mortals. They took captives off to their sabbats and revelries.

The Wild Hunt actually rode out every night, but it was especially strong on the nights of the full moon and was the worst and most dangerous on pagan holidays. People tried to protect themselves by making the sign of the cross at the entrances to their homes and barns and leaving offerings of food. It was wise to stay indoors and let the shrieking mob pass by.

THE *SLUAGH*

In Scottish Highland lore, the fairy members of the Wild Hunt are the *Sluagh*, also known as the Host and the Unforgiven Dead, the most wicked fairies of all. The *Sluagh* are the souls of the unbaptized dead and also the souls of violent men who killed others during their lives. In some accounts they are fallen angels.

The *Sluagh* fly in great swarms high in the air every night, especially around midnight. They fight each other, and their blood falls like rain onto the earth. Bright red lichen called *crotal* is said to be the gelled blood of these fairies.

When not slaughtering each other, the *Sluagh* swoop down and capture mortals who are foolish enough to be out on Walpurgisnacht. They carry their victims over both land and sea, then drop them into mud and bogs, sometimes killing them.[3] One account from Scotland tells of a child snatched up one night. It was returned the next day, lifeless, with the palms of its hands stuck into holes in the walls of its house.

The *Sluagh* also force their captives to be slaves and to shoot their poisonous, fatal, elf-shot arrows into humans and animals. In earlier times they targeted women milking cows and anyone working at night. Sometimes their captives were able to shoot animals instead of fellow mortals, such as in the following account from Scotland:

> There was a man who had only one cow and one daughter. The daughter was milking the cow at night when the hosts were passing, and the human being whom the hosts had lifted with them was her father's neighbor. And this neighbor was ordered by the hosts to shoot the daughter as she was milking, but, knowing the father and daughter, he shot the cow instead. The next morning he went where the father was and said to him, "You are missing the cow." "Yes," said the father, "I am." And the man who had shot the cow said, "Are you not glad your cow and not your daughter

was *taken*? For I was ordered to shoot your daughter and I shot your cow in order to show blood on my arrow." "I am very glad of what you have done if that was the case," the father replied. "It was the case," the neighbor said.[4]

The *Sluagh* also take cattle for their food. When they have consumed all the meat, they take the hides and roll up old men in them, and drop them to the ground. The flying fairies, abductions of humans and cattle, and sickening of people and animals have similarities to the activities of extraterrestrials, explored in a later chapter.

TRICKSTER TRAVEL GUIDES

Among the most common of the bad fairies found around the world are those that like to lead travelers astray, especially at night. Some of them, like the pixies of Cornwall, England, are not malevolent, but they are more prone to harming people than helping them. Others are out-and-out nasty.

These lethal travel guides are known by various names. The **Will-o-the-Wisp**, Will-o-the-Wykes, and Will-o-Wisp appear in British Isles lore. They are mysterious bobbing lights known as *ignis fatuus*, which means "foolish fire."[5] It is foolish to follow them, for disaster results.

In the days before highways were lit with electricity, it was easy to become lost at night. The bobbing fairy lights seemed to beckon lost travelers, leading them across dark terrain. But their destination turned out to be a lake, bog, or swamp where travelers could be injured or killed. At the very least they might be led in circles or deeper into unknown territory.

Bobbing night lights are also called corpse candles, for it is bad luck to see them, and they portend death within a year.

One modern explanation given for the lights is glowing marsh and swamp gas, which can appear to bob, weave, and move in the darkness. Swamp gas is the product of decaying vegetation, which catches fire spontaneously under certain conditions and glows in the dark.

WATER HORSES

More dangerous still to travelers are water horses and water maidens, fairies that inhabit lakes, rivers, and streams. In Scotland, the kelpies are half human and half horse in shape, and can shape-shift into the form of a shaggy, dark man. A kelpie can leap onto the horseback of a traveler and either crush him or drag him and his horse into waters to drown. Kelpies also are fond of kidnapping women and children and dragging them into the watery depths of their lairs.

In storms the kelpies yelp, howl, and thrash the water with their mighty tails, making the sound of thunder.

It is a mistake to challenge a kelpie. One story tells that a man named Graham of Morphie, Scotland, once bridled a kelpie and forced it to build his castle. When it was done, he freed the kelpie, but it cursed him as it raced back into the water. From then on, Graham of Morphie and his family had nothing but misfortune for the rest of their lives.[6]

Figure 6.1   *A water kelpie takes a passing gentleman by surprise. Kelpies generally frequent Scottish waters and often appear in human or equine form.* (Mary Evans Picture Library/The Image Works)

To see a kelpie means death by drowning, and nothing can prevent it from happening. A story is told in lore about such a case. A group of reapers in a field saw a kelpie in the form of a beautiful water nymph in a false ford in a river. The kelpie called out, "The hour is come but not the man," and dove into the water. Just then a man on horseback galloped up as though to rescue what he thought was a drowning woman. The reapers halted the horse and forced the man to the local church, telling him to wait until after the "ill hour." But when they returned, they found the man dead inside the church. The kelpie's forecast of doom was not to be thwarted.[7]

RED CAP

Some wicked fairies are like vampires. They like human blood. Red Cap is a small, wizened fairy whose cap is red because it is stained with the blood of his victims. He is a short, thickset old man, with long prominent teeth, skinny fingers with talons like eagles, large fiery red eyes, hair streaming down his shoulders, iron boots, a pike-staff in his left hand, and, of course, a red cap on his head. He lives in old, ruined castles and peel towers in the borderlands between England and Scotland and attacks unwary visitors. He is far stronger than he appears, and the best way to ward him off is by making the sign of the cross.[8]

THE BANSHEE

The **banshee** is a death omen fairy, a hag-like woman who appears dressed in white or red or gray, and wails to forecast the death of a person. She flies through the air or stands in front of a window of a home and cries mournfully.

The appearance and purpose of this fairy may seem malevolent, but in fact, the banshee is simply a messenger. She does not cause death but announces it. She is associated with families; in Scottish and

Figure 6.2 *Two banshees hover above a boat, forecasting the death of one of its passengers.* (Vladimir Egorovic Makovsky/Getty Images)

Trolls

Trolls are among the worst of the bad boys in Fairyland. In Scandinavian and northern European lore they are a type of dwarf, uglier than most other dwarfs and fairies. They have mean-looking faces and are short, squat, and stumpy. They have long, crooked noses and big humps on their backs. While other fairies dress in beautiful, colorful clothing, trolls wear dull gray outfits and red caps with long points.

Trolls are excellent metalworkers and can be heard hammering inside of their hills.

Many fairies steal from humans, and trolls reign as the best thieves, which may account for them being among the richest of fairies. They will steal anything, including women and children.

Trolls have many magical powers. They can make themselves invisible or shape-shift into any desired form. They can bestow riches on humans or create misfortune for them. They possess supernormal strength, which they can bestow upon humans.

Some trolls live beneath bridges and take great delight in attacking travelers. In earlier times they rushed out to spook horses and beat up foot travelers. Today they are reputed to cause motor vehicle accidents.

There are two ways to deal with bridge trolls. One is to avoid bridges, which is nearly impossible in many places today. The next best defense is to say a prayer of protection right before crossing the bridge.

Irish lore, families whose names begin with "Mac" and "O'" have their personal banshee who makes these grim announcements.

In Gaelic the banshee is spelled *bean si*, which means "fairy woman." The fairy is also known as *bean-nighe* (ben-neeyeh), or "the Washing Woman."[9] She is a small fairy woman dressed in green who is seen by the banks of remote streams, washing the blood-stained clothing of people who are about to die. In some accounts she is the ghost of a woman who died in childbirth. If she is interrupted in her washing, she will take her bloody linens and strike the person on the legs, rendering them paralyzed.

To see the Washing Woman forecasts evil and misfortune, but if a person can get between her and the water, she will be forced to answer three questions truthfully or grant three wishes.

7

Changelings

A young Scottish farmer man and his wife are thrilled when their first child is born, a boy they name Johnny. As time passes, however, they wonder if something is wrong with their infant. He doesn't grow, he cries all the time, and he is never satisfied with anything.

One day the couple goes to market and asks their neighbor, a tailor, to watch the child. The tailor sits by the fire sewing and is startled when a voice says, "Is my mother and my father away?" The voice couldn't possibly belong to the baby, so the tailor ignores it. The voice repeats the question. He looks at Johnny and sees the child sitting up and gripping the sides of the cradle.

Before the tailor can recover, Johnny says, "There's a bottle of whiskey in the press. Give us a drink."

The tailor fetches the whiskey and the two of them drink. Johnny then tells the tailor to fetch him some pipes, and he plays beautiful music.

When Johnny's parents come home, all the child says are baby sounds like "nya nya nya."

The tailor realizes that the boy is a **changeling**, a fairy child. The fairies have stolen the couple's real boy. He informs the farmer. They set a trap. The next day the parents pretend to be away, but hide where they can watch Johnny. The child gives a repeat performance.

Faced with this proof, the farmer gets a bag of horse manure, goes into the house, and heats it up on the stove, intending to drive away the fairy child with the stink. The changeling shoots up the chimney and escapes.[1]

In earlier times one of the biggest threats posed by fairies was their kidnapping of human children. Fairy children were ugly and sickly, it was believed, and the fairies prized beautiful human babies. But they didn't only take the human children; they substituted their own in their place.

Stories in both folk tales and personal experience have similar themes. Sometimes the parents know right away that they have a changeling, because it is ugly, hairy, or even demonic in appearance. It may have a large humpback or is shriveled and misshapen in other ways. It doesn't grow properly and has a poor appetite.

In other cases the parents suspect they have been given a changeling but are not sure. The baby looks very much like theirs, but he or she is strangely different, not right. Tests were given to prove the true identity of the baby. If the child could be made to talk or laugh, it would reveal itself.

One common test was the "brewery of eggshells." The child was placed before the hearth fire, and a row of eggshells filled with water was set on the fire. When the water boiled, a changeling would talk and laugh in wonder. The child would exclaim something like, "I have lived 800 years and I have never seen the like of that before!" or "I am as old was the Westerwald but I've never seen anyone cooking in an eggshell!" or "I have seen the acorn before the oak: I have seen the egg before the white chicken: I have never seen the equal to this!"[2]

Often the human parents could get their child back through drastic measures. They either had to beat the changeling or threaten to beat it. The fairies would hear and would come quickly with the kidnapped human child. The parents might also take the changeling to a fairy mound and leave it.

Sometimes the changelings disappeared once they were exposed, but the sad parents never got their own baby back. In other cases the mortals had to search for their child and rescue it from Fairyland.

Figure 7.1 *A group of fairies snatches a human baby from its mother. Fairies sometimes abduct human babies and leave fairy offspring in their place.* (Fortean Picture Library)

TEEN CHANGELINGS

Changelings were usually small infants, but the kidnapping and exchange could take place at any age. A Scottish Highlands story tells about a boy of 14 who was kidnapped and traded. The boy was the only son of a blacksmith, who was a widower. He was a bright and

Figure 7.2 *A man detects a changeling when he brews beer in eggshells.* (Mary Evans Picture Library/The Image Works)

happy lad, always willing to help his father in his work.

One day the boy underwent a mysterious change. He took to his bed and was silent. No matter how much he ate, he grew thinner and thinner. His skin yellowed and aged until he looked like a sick old man. His worried father was certain he was going to die.

A friend came to visit and recognized right away that this boy was really a changeling. The father administered the eggshell test and the changeling was exposed when he laughed and shouted. The blacksmith built a great fire, intending to throw the changeling into it, but the fairy escaped up the chimney.

The fairies did not return the mortal son, so the father was determined to find and rescue him. On the night of the full moon, he went out to the fairy hill, armed with a Bible, a living cock, and a dirk (a type of knife). He stuck his dirk into the hill, which opened the door to the mound. He entered and found himself in Fairyland, where all the fairies were dancing and feasting. In a corner working at a forge was a group of slaves, including his son.

Upon seeing the blacksmith the fairies became angry. They tried to shut the access to the hill, but the door with the dirk in it would not close. The fairies swarmed about the man, demanding to know what he wanted. When he replied that he wanted his son back, the fairies screamed and shouted at him, but they could not touch or enchant him because of the Bible.

The noise awakened the cock, which climbed onto the blacksmith's shoulder and crowed. Fairies are in the habit of scattering when a cock

Married to Fairies

Besides pretty children, fairies also are attracted to pretty adults. Some fall in love with humans and marry them, creating hybrid children. If the desired mortals cannot be enticed willingly to Fairyland for a wedding, the fairies resort to enchantment, and kidnap them, such as in the account of Thomas the Rhymer.

Mortals also fall in love with fairies and go to great lengths to woo them to marriage, for fairies spouses bestow great blessings. Fairy brides and wives are more common than fairy husbands. A mortal man comes upon a beautiful female fairy and convinces her to marry him and live in the land of humans.

Fairy marriages can be happy, such as the story about a poor girl who one day heard a dwarf hammering away inside a hill, singing while he did his metalwork. She told him she wished she could sing like him and live underground like him. The dwarf immediately proposed marriage and a share of his great wealth. The girl accepted and lived happily ever after with her attentive dwarf husband.[3]

In some cases the mortal spouses live under a warning that certain conditions must be met or certain things must never happen, lest the fairy spouses vanish. There are many stories of fairy brides who warn that they will disappear if their husbands strike them three times, no matter what the reason, or if their husbands rebuke them in front of their fairy families. The taboos are usually broken and so are the marriages and all the prosperity that went with them. There are no second chances with fairies!

crows, for it means dawn is coming. When the fairies fled, the farmer grabbed his son, and they escaped out the open door.

The boy was not himself for a year and a day, and then the fairies' enchantment ended. He resumed his old personality.[4]

PROTECTION AGAINST FAIRY-NAPPING

Fairies stole children at any time, but they usually came at night when everyone in a household was fast asleep. It was impossible to guard a child around the clock, so other remedies were used to keep fairies away. Iron scissors or nails were placed beneath an infant's pillow or hung around a cradle. The iron repelled fairies and weakened their powers. A sprig of boxwood blessed on Palm Sunday had the same effect. In addition, parents said prayers of protection.

EXPLANATIONS FOR CHANGELINGS

According to modern views, changelings may have explained unpleasant but natural conditions in infants. Babies actually born with deformities or congenital defects were said to be exchanged immediately or soon after birth. Sometimes congenital defects might not show up until a baby was older and was obviously not developing properly. If a child died unexpectedly—from what today is called Sudden Infant Death Syndrome—parents might believe that the fairies actually took their child and left behind a changeling who died.

Changelings also could have explained "good children gone bad," older children who did not behave well or who even committed crimes.

Finally, it must be considered that changelings were what people believed them to be: fairy children.

An account of changelings who were social problems comes from nineteenth-century France. The oldest son of a family in the village of Kergoff was born a pretty child. One day the mother discovered that during the night the pretty baby was gone and a hideous, hunchbacked, dark child was now in the cradle. The parents raised the changeling, who grew up to be "demonic." He was full of vices and tried several times to murder the mother. People fled from him.

The woman had two other children, a boy and a girl, who also were stolen by the fairies. The second boy changeling was hunchbacked, and the girl was so deformed that she looked like a ball. She was the terror of the village, and the second son also was bad.

When the mother became pregnant a fourth time, she took the advice of a wise woman and placed boxwood in the cradle. The fairies came no more.[5]

The Extraterrestrial Connection

In the early nineteenth century, David Williams, a Welsh servant, is out at night, walking behind his mistress and carrying a load of bacon. He has a strange experience that causes him to arrive home three hours later than his mistress.

According to his story, he saw a flash of light in the sky followed by a hoop of fire that descended to earth. A small man and woman, both well-dressed, got out of the hoop and traced a circle on the ground. Immediately a large number of small men and women appeared and danced around the ring to the sweetest music Williams had ever heard. Entranced, he watched them.

At some point—it seemed like only a few minutes later—the meteor-like flash of light appeared in the sky again, and the hoop of fire descended. Then the little men and women jumped into the hoop and disappeared. Williams finds himself alone in the darkness, and makes his way home three hours late.[1]

Did Williams witness fairies or extraterrestrials (ETs)? The beings descended from the sky like ETs but acted like fairies. In the early nineteenth century, visitors from space were unheard of. People did not talk about unidentified flying objects. The only interpretation obvious at the time was fairies, which were believed to travel in the sky.

A REEXAMINATION OF FAIRIES

Modern ufology began in 1947, when a pilot named Kenneth Arnold saw strange shining crafts in the sky while he was flying near Mt. Rainier in Washington State. He said they skipped through the air like saucers, and the term *flying saucers* was born. Soon after that, in the 1950s, people began reporting sightings of, and encounters with, strange little beings that landed in mysterious crafts.

Ufologists and folklorists familiar with fairy lore noticed the striking similarities in descriptions of fairies and ETs. Could it be possible that the beings were the same? Perhaps humans were interpreting them differently, in accordance with changes in technology and the times. Folklorist Thomas E. Bullard, of Indiana, has stated that aliens and fairies are virtually identical save for a "change of address and mode of transportation."[2] Ufologist Jacques Vallee also has drawn many comparisons between fairies and ETs. The similarities certainly raise questions about the true nature and origins of both.

LITTLE FOLK

Many descriptions of fairies tell of small humanoids, two to five feet in height. They are frequently described as wearing red caps and either red, green or gray clothing. Sometimes their clothing looks like military uniforms.

ET contact accounts are full of descriptions of little people in similar clothing. On November 1, 1954, a woman was going to visit a grave in a cemetery in Poggio d'Ambra, Italy. She was carrying a pot of flowers. En route she spied a torpedo-shaped, metallic-looking craft unlike anything she had ever seen before. As she stared at it, two little beings about two-and-a-half to three feet tall came out from behind the craft. They were wearing gray coveralls and red leather helmets that reminded the woman of military garb. They had thin white teeth that showed as they smiled. The beings seemed "joyful" and playful.

Chattering in an unknown language, they came up to her and took away her pot of flowers. She screamed and ran away. She returned to the scene with other people, but the craft and the beings had vanished—along with her flowers.[3]

SPECIAL POWERS

Both fairies and ETs display supernormal powers. They have the ability to be invisible, to walk through solid objects such as walls, and to levitate into the air. They render humans unable to move, and they possess unusual strength. They have psychic abilities and healing powers. They offer prophecies of the future.

MISSING TIME

Time passes slowly in Fairyland. People who stumble into the place or who fall under fairy enchantment, like David Williams above, discover they have experienced missing time. For them, a short amount of time passes. They are astonished to find that, in some cases, months or years of mortal time have passed instead.

Some people who encounter ETs also have missing time. The first dramatic case of ET missing time occurred in 1961, when Betty and Barney Hill encountered a landed craft while driving late at night in New Hampshire. They lost awareness, and the next thing they knew, they were driving home again—with two hours unaccounted for. Under hypnosis, they recalled being taken aboard an alien craft and subjected to medical examinations.

In 1975 another famous missing time case took place. A logger named Travis Walton went missing for five days after being zapped by a beam of light from a hovering craft. His companions fled, and when they returned to the scene, Walton was gone. He turned up later in another town, disoriented and disheveled, thinking he had been gone only a short time.

ABDUCTIONS

The Hills and Walton also experienced abductions, another similarity between fairies and ETs. Fairies abduct people by enchanting them and levitating them off to Fairyland. ETs abduct by taking people in their sleep, or paralyzing them, and levitating them to their ships. In both cases the humans are held captive as long as the abductors wish. When they are returned to ordinary reality, they are dazed and confused, and sometimes find themselves in a different location than where they were abducted.

CHANGELINGS AND HYBRIDS

Fairies and ETs share an intense interest in human offspring. The fairies take human children and leave their own sickly babies in place. The ETs want to create hybrid human-alien offspring. Abductees say they have been told that ET babies are sickly, and their races are in need of new genetic material.

Fairies created hybrids, too, by marrying humans. There are few accounts of alien marriages, but many abductees report having sexual encounters with their captors.

FAIRY RINGS AND SAUCER NESTS

Fairies leave rings behind them where they have danced. The rings are marked by mushrooms (used by the fairies for seats) and by flattened and dead grass. According to some lore, nothing will grow in the circles touched by fairy feet. Grass and vegetation will grow in the center of the ring and outside it, but not in the ring track itself.

A similar phenomenon has been noted about the alleged landing places of ET spacecraft, many of which are round in shape. "Saucer nests," circular areas of flattened vegetation, have been reported around the world in connection with sightings of mysterious lights and craft. The vegetation within the circle is burned, yellowed, or sometimes covered with a greasy substance that soon kills the grass. The vegetation—grass or crops—is often flattened in a clockwise direction or is moved or even removed. Nothing grows inside the circle for a long time.

For example, in the 1960s a wave of UFO sightings in Australia were accompanied by discoveries of saucer nests. Three nests were found on January 23, 1966, in a swampy area in Queensland, where a spinning metallic craft had been seen rising up off the water. Reeds were flattened in a clockwise direction in two of the nests and counterclockwise in the third. The nests ranged from eight to 30 feet in diameter. The reeds inside the nest were dead.[4]

On November 12, 1968, a saucer nest discovered near Necochea, Brazil, had eight giant white mushrooms measuring three feet in diameter growing inside it.

Figure 8.1 *A saucer nest embedded in the ground in Canada in September 1974. Some people see a link between such nests and the rings left on the ground by fairies.* (Mary Evans Picture Library/The Image Works)

ATTACKS ON ANIMALS AND PEOPLE

Wicked fairies made elf-shot, poisonous arrows that were shot into animals and humans, who sickened and died. Some fairies also have a

The Hopkinsville Terrors

In 1955 rural southwestern Kentucky was a sleepy place where nothing much unusual happened. On the night of August 21, one family was thrust into a nightmare when little goblin-like creatures from a UFO held them under siege.

Billy Ray Taylor was visiting his friends the Sutton family at their farm located between Kelly and Hopkinsville. Around 7:00 p.m. on August 21, he went outside to fetch water from the well and saw a shining object land in a gully nearby. Soon the family dog was barking.

Taylor and Carl Sutton grabbed their guns and went outside to investigate. They were astonished to see a creature about three to four feet tall walking toward them. It had large round eyes, large pointy ears, skinny legs, hands with claws, and a thin, slit-like mouth. They fired their guns point blank into the creature. Unharmed, it did a back flip and ran into the woods.

The men returned to the house. The same creature, or another one looking just like it, peered in a window. They fired at it and then went outside to see if they had killed it. The creature was up on the roof, and it reached down to touch their hair. They fired at it again, but it floated to the ground and ran off into the woods.

So began the siege. Multiple creatures all looking alike jumped up and down on the roof and peered into the windows, as though intensely curious. The men fired and fired but never seemed to harm any of the beings.

After about three hours the terrified people dashed to their vehicles and tore down the road to the Hopkinsville police. The officers on duty laughed at their story but finally agreed to come out to the farm. When they got there, no creatures were to be seen.

taste for human blood. ETs have been associated with animal mutilations. Their "elf-shot" are not arrows but deadly beams of light, usually red (a color favored by fairies) that they shoot from their craft. In

Figure 8.2 *At the Sutton farm near Hopkinsville, Kentucky, eight adults and three children were terrorized by small glowing creatures that were immune to gunshots. The creatures appeared shortly after a UFO was spotted landing nearby.* (Mary Evans Picture Library/The Image Works)

As soon as the officers left, the little tricksters came back, tormenting the family until just before sunrise. The police returned, along with representatives of the U.S. Air Force, but no evidence of the creatures could be found. They had left as mysteriously as they had arrived.

The creatures resembled beings described in fairy accounts, yet their arrival coincided with the sighting of a UFO. Fairies or space aliens? No one will ever know.

South America these lethal craft are called *chupa-chupas*, or "suckers." Victims believe they are sucked of their vital energy or blood.

From July 1977 to November 1978, a wave of deadly UFO activity around Colares, Brazil, killed people and at least one animal—a dog—and left others seriously ill. In all, about 40 people, most of them adults, received medical treatment for injuries. Most of the victims were struck by mysterious beams of red light that severely burned their chests. Blood tests showed the victims to have abnormally low levels of hemoglobin. Some of the victims did not die directly from the burns but suffered a wasting away over a period of months and then died. One victim likened the feeling to being pierced with a needle, which is similar to the pricks people felt when they were elf-shot by fairies.[5]

HEALING AND PROPHECY

When fairies choose, they have the power to bestow the gift of healing and prophecy upon people, as they did with Thomas the Rhymer. ETs who are benevolent tell contactees that they have come to help human beings in various ways, such as healing of illnesses. The ETs show people visions of the future and make dire predictions for the human race and the planet if people do not mend their ways.

A NEW MYTHOLOGY

Since the late 1980s, the media and entertainment industries have served up one image of ETs that now dominates public conceptions of them: a small, hairless, bug-eyed "gray" that abducts humans. In fact, the descriptions of ETs are far more varied. Thousands upon thousands of ET cases have been documented, and the descriptions of the beings seem more like a who's who from Fairyland: they are all shapes and sizes, humanoid and not, hairy and hairless.

The remarkable similarities between fairies and ETs calls for deeper investigation of what human beings may actually be experiencing.

The evidence points to the possibility of genuine contact with beings from other realms, but what is their true identity? Perhaps it is neither fairies nor ETs but something else. Vallee states that a new mythology may be in the making.[6] The answers may never be sorted out, but a re-examination of otherworldly encounters may lead to a new perspective on humanity's place in the universe.

How to See Fairies

Amanda enjoys working in her garden. She is surprised one day to discover that she is not alone there; she has company, and it isn't human or animal. At first she doesn't believe her eyes.

She is weeding one of her little flower beds when she becomes aware of a small figure standing between rhododendron bushes. It looks like a little man about two to three feet high. She sees it first out of the corner of her eye, and when she looks directly at it, it vanishes. Then it reappears when she looks away.

Through her side vision, Amanda sees more detail. To her astonishment, the little man is nothing like she has ever seen before. He is human-like in shape and has a human-like face, but his skin is a mottled green and brown, and his hair looks like a tangle of twigs. It is as though he is made of vegetation. Amanda wonders if she is seeing things with her imagination. After a while, the little man disappears.

The next time she works in the garden, he comes back. Soon she realizes that he responds to her thoughts, and so she sends him a mental greeting. After that, she sees the little man often and notices that he moves quickly among the flowers and bushes, as though he is a gardener's helper. She has the impression he is happy, not only with her garden but with her efforts in it. Everything in her garden grows exceptionally well.[1]

In earlier times, few people wanted to see fairies, for it was widely believed that the little folk would not be pleased to be noticed. Bad

Figure 9.1 *A little girl encounters a caravan of fairies at the bottom of her garden.* (Mary Evans Picture Library/Douglas McCarthy/The Image Works)

luck might follow if the fairies caught a person watching them. If people realized fairies were present and doing work for them, it was said, it was best to leave them alone, but make sure to compensate them in some way.

Attitudes have changed. Now many people want to see fairies and even to communicate and work with them in nature and eco-friendly projects. It seems the little folk have modified their attitudes as well, for people report pleasant and beneficial experiences with them.[2]

In the past people believed that fairies were invisible unless they chose to let a person see them. They could also be seen by accident, while people were busy doing their chores or traveling. The following story occurred in 2006 to a young woman driving along a remote country road late at night. The fairy, a small, winged being, seemed to deliberately reveal itself:

> I was driving on a dark dirt road in New England around midnight, with no lights of any kind except car headlights. At first I was not certain what I was seeing. Floating slowly in front of the windshield was an ultra blue light, about eight inches long and about two or three inches wide.
>
> As soon as I recognized this odd light, it stopped floating and stood in front of the windshield very still as I was driving along. Then to my amazement, a fairy appeared—very humanlike but tiny, with beautiful wings that were transparent and an off-white color, with a design on the upper parts. She wore clothes but no shoes. I saw her tiny feet. She had blonde hair and was very cute. She turned her head to look at me and smiled.
>
> I could not believe what I saw. I actually bent myself forward real close to the windshield and rubbed my eyes, thinking I was tired and was seeing things. But I did see her, and she remained in front of the windshield for about five minutes. Then she slowly drifted away towards the

left of the windshield on my driving side. She didn't disappear, she just drifted away.

I have mentioned this to a chosen few people. Some believe that I was imagining, others listen with curiosity. It didn't bother me that some chose not to believe, for at first I didn't either.

The memory of this cute fairy is vivid in my mind and I have drawn her exactly as she was. I will never reveal where I saw this fairy for fear she would be hunted and possibly hurt, so I shall keep it a secret until I leave this earth. I consider myself very fortunate to have seen such an amazing creature that most would say doesn't exist.[3]

This young woman was in the right place at the right time and in the right frame of mind. She was pleasantly distracted while driving, not thinking intensely about anything. She may never know the reason why the fairy appeared to her. Perhaps it was to open her eyes and awareness to them, so that she could see them again, or begin a study of them—or even educate other people about them.

In folklore, a four-leaf clover is believed to give "**fairy sight**" to the holder, as well as protect the person against unwanted enchantments. The fairies also give the gift of seeing them with a magical ointment rubbed on the eyes.

It is difficult to know from records exactly how people saw fairies in earlier times. Did they see them literally, with their physical eyes, or mentally, as impressions on the mind? Most accounts in folklore indicate that people felt they saw fairies with their physical eyes. In many cases, there were multiple witnesses to the same sights.

Fairies are still seen this way, and they are also perceived by the inner eye as a mental impression. Some people think their mental impressions are tricks of the imagination, but this is a genuine way that paranormal phenomena—things that are invisible—can be noticed. Seeing the invisible either way is part of a psychic ability called clairvoyance, or "clear seeing."

Fairy sight, or the Sight, as it was called in the past, actually involves more than vision. All the senses combine for psychic awareness. In addition to mental visual impressions, the Sight involves sensations on the skin, sounds, smells, and even tastes.

ANYONE CAN LEARN TO SEE FAIRIES

Special psychic gifts aren't necessary to see fairies. Attitude and openness are more important. For those willing to believe and to respect what they see, the fairy realms may reveal themselves. Fairies also respond to people who respect the natural world, who are able to "see" the vibrant life in the plants, trees, earth, water, and air. Fairies will know those who enjoy spending time in nature and see it as a temple of life and be attracted to them.

Fairies often appear when a person feels in harmony with the environment. Those interested in experiencing fairies should think of a time when they were outdoors, such as on a camping trip or a hike, and they looked around at the beautiful scenery and maybe felt awestruck. That's a state of mind and emotion that can bring the fairies forward. They are around people all the time, but humans don't notice them except at special moments. It is possible for many people to increase those moments through practice, rather than waiting for them to happen by chance.

To see fairies, one should have the right intention, be able to relax, and have a good imagination. An attitude of playfulness helps, too. Perhaps that is one reason why fairies gravitate to children and young people; they know how to play.

HOW TO DEVELOP FAIRY SIGHT

Set aside a few minutes every day, or as often as possible, to relax in a meditative way. If you can, try it outdoors. There are plenty of fairies in cities and indoors, however, so practice anyway, if you do not have access to a yard or a park. Relax your mind by letting go of your

Figure 9.2 *Fairies can sometimes be perceived as small, twinkling lights in wilderness environments.* (Adam Weiss/Getty Images)

thoughts and concerns. One way to do that is to think of something that makes you happy, and concentrate on the feeling of happiness. A few deep breaths will also help you to relax physically.

Pay attention to your environment. Notice the breeze and the way plants move in it. Notice birds, clouds, shapes, and colors. Pay attention to sounds. In this way, you will tune in to the subtle energies of nature that exist below the level of ordinary awareness. Most of the time, people are too busy with activities in daily life to experience the subtle life that goes on around them.

Build your intention to see fairies. You can accomplish this by reading about them and by asking mentally to see them. It is important to have the right intention, such as a desire to advance your knowledge rather than to be entertained.

Be patient. You may feel that nothing happens right away. It may take some time to open fairy sight. Also, fairies seldom make dramatic appearances. Instead, they quietly materialize, and they may be visible for only a few seconds.[4]

Dusk and dawn are good times to look for fairies. The subdued light makes then easier to see.

WHAT DO YOU EXPERIENCE?

Try not to have preset expectations of what fairies should look like. They come in many shapes and forms. One of the most common is not a human shape, but a ball of sparkling light that moves quickly.

Gifts That Please Fairies

Fairies love to have their presence and work acknowledged. They enjoy human appreciation, but even more they like gifts of food and sometimes objects. If you wish to strengthen your ability to see and perhaps communicate with fairies, try leaving gifts out for them at home or in the yard or garden.

The best offerings are sweet foods and drink, such as cream or milk sweetened with honey, cookies, cakes, and chocolate. Leave small quantities on a saucer. The fairies will not take the food itself, but will take the essence of it. Never eat anything left for the fairies, for once they "eat" it themselves, it loses its nutritional value. According to lore, fairy-eaten food will even sicken people and animals.

Fairies like shiny objects, so try small trinkets, toys, and fairy ornaments. Never leave money. Fairies have a great deal of pride and they will be insulted that their services are being "bought."

Some people set up a special place for fairy offerings, such as in a corner of a room or a special spot in a garden.

The lights come in different sizes and colors. Some of the lights are tiny and twinkling, like carpets of light laid on the ground. Or, you may see little, human-like beings. Some people see fairies as ripples of light.

You may see fairies better out of the corners of your eyes rather than by looking directly at them.

You may not have significant visual images, but instead experience fairies as a presence that you feel. Pay attention to physical cues such as a tingling of the skin or a peculiar buzzing in the ears. These are often ways that people become aware of an unseen presence.

Fairies may communicate but not in words. Instead, you may get impressions, such as feelings or thoughts that pop into your head. For example, they may convey that they are happy to see you, or they are happy in their environment.

SHOW APPRECIATION

Tell the fairies "thank you" if they visit. Even if you don't perceive them, say thanks anyway, in case little invisibles are listening. The best way to show appreciation is to take care of your home and respect the natural world.

10

Enchanted Gardens,
Enchanted World

Molly Sheehan is out gardening one day in her pride and joy, Green Hope Farm, in Meriden, New Hampshire. She is completely immersed in the joy of working the earth. Ever since childhood, she has felt a strong affinity with nature and nature spirits. Green Hope Farm is where her dream is coming true, to cultivate flowers and produce in close cooperation with the spirit of Nature itself.

Today something new happens. As she works away, she becomes aware that she is getting "little messages" that come into her thoughts. It seems as though the plants are talking to her. The asparagus has something to say. So do the flowers. It's not her imagination! Who is speaking?[1]

A NEW WAY TO GARDEN

Sheehan paid attention to the messages, which were advice on how to cultivate the farm. They told her what, how, and when to plant, how to cultivate, and also how to design gardens. The more she paid attention, the more the messages increased. What was more, the advice was sound. If she followed it, she got results.

Sheehan felt she had tuned into the voices of the beings that are part of nature and help the growth of vegetation. Are they angels,

devas, fairies, or elementals? Sheehan resists putting a label on the beings, feeling that any name does not properly describe who they are. They are more like a spectrum of energy. She senses them by their spiritual vibrations.

Initially, Sheehan spent hours in meditation in order to communicate with her unseen partners. Over the years, she perfected her ability so that communication is much easier. It flows naturally, like intuition.

The purpose of Green Hope Farm is to demonstrate how the angelic, elemental, and human kingdoms can work harmoniously together and with God, according to Sheehan.

The nature beings emphasized the importance of the shapes of gardens and communicated instructions for specific designs. The geometric shape of a garden determines the spiritual energies that will grow into the plants.

Green Hope Farm has become renowned for its flower essences. The essences are distilled liquids made from harvested flowers said to contain certain spiritual and healing properties. The essences are taken like homeopathic remedies: a few drops mixed in liquids or placed under the tongue. The spiritual and healing properties are cultivated into the plants with the help of the nature realm.

Sheehan once thought that only special people could talk to angels and nature spirits. Now she knows that everyone can learn to communicate with them. "Imagination is the bridge across," she says. "Things that we think are our imagination are really messages. The more attention I paid to the messages, the more I realized that we always channel—we are always connected."[2] Sheehan sees the partnership between realms as an exciting adventure for the angels and elementals, too, not just for humans.

Green Hope Farm is but one of many farm and garden communities dedicated to sustainable living and eco-green policies. At some of them, cooperation with nature spirits is acknowledged as an important part of their success. Some communities do not publicize these human-fairy relationships but prefer to emphasize their "green" work.

Perelandra, located near Jeffersonton, Virginia, is another garden and nature research center that had its beginnings in communication with angelic and nature spirits. Founded in the 1970s by Maechelle Small Wright and Clarence Wright, Perelandra offers products, workshops, and resources for sustainable, green gardening and farming.

The name "Perelandra" comes from the title of a science fiction novel by C.S. Lewis. The story takes place on Venus, called Perelandra, the planet of perfection. It is visited by two Earth men, one good and the other evil. The good man moved within the harmony of Perelandra, while the evil man moved in destruction. Perelandra symbolizes the need to be in harmony with the environment in order to achieve perfection.

FINDHORN: A PLANETARY LIGHT COMMUNITY

The mother of all modern green communities is Findhorn, founded in northern Scotland near the Arctic Circle in the 1960s. Findhorn sits on a once-inhospitable piece of land along the North Sea. With the help of nature spirits, Findhorn produced amazing crops and became an international magnet for spiritual seekers.

In 1962 Peter and Eileen Caddy and their friend, Dorothy Maclean, were out of work. They went to live cheaply in a trailer park at Findhorn. All three of them were steeped in meditation and spiritual study. Maclean was especially gifted as a psychic and channeler.

To pass the time, Peter tried his hand at gardening, with limited success. Findhorn seemed the worst place imaginable to grow anything. The soil was sandy, and the land was exposed to near-constant winds from all sides. Peter kept on trying, and the three of them meditated every day.

In May 1963 Maclean received an unusual message from a spirit about the "forces of Nature." The spirit told her that it was her job to attune to and harmonize with those forces, which would in turn welcome her into their world. Peter believed the message meant that they could get guidance on what to do in the garden. The spirit communicator quickly agreed, telling Maclean:

> Yes, you can cooperate in the garden. Begin by thinking about the nature spirits, the higher overlighting nature spirits, and tune into them. That will be so unusual as to draw their interest here. They will be overjoyed to find some members of the human race eager for their help.
>
> By the higher nature spirits I mean the spirits of differing physical forms such as clouds, rain, vegetables. The smaller individual nature spirits are under their jurisdiction. In the new world to come these realms will be open to humans—or should I say, humans will be open to them. Just be open and seek into the glorious realms of Nature with sympathy and understanding, knowing that these beings are of the Light, willing to help but suspicious of humans and on the lookout for the false. Keep with me and they will not find it, and you will all build towards the new.[3]

Maclean followed the instructions. The first nature spirit to come into her awareness was what she called the "Pea Deva," which she described as holding the pattern for all the peas in the world. Her main contact was the "Landscape Angel," who had a broad outlook and brought in other spirits for communication.

Initially, Maclean did not know what to call the beings. She did not like the religious associations with the term "angel." She settled on "deva," a Sanskrit term meaning "shining ones." The beings she saw in her mind's eyes were big and shining. Maclean went on to use the terms *angel*, *deva*, and *nature spirit* interchangeably. Later in life, she felt that "angel" better expressed the beings she experienced. Others who have had similar experiences feel "fairy" or "nature spirit" are the best terms.

With the advice of the devas (Maclean's favored term during her Findhorn years), Peter's garden flourished and overflowed with produce. Cabbages, normally about four pounds in weight, were over 40

A Celebration of Fairies

Every year in spring and summer, huge festivals take place around the world in celebration of fairies. People come in costume to dance, sing, learn about fairies, and shop for all kinds of fairy-themed merchandise. Similar to Renaissance fairs, the fairy festivals are usually held outdoors.

Fairies have indeed come a long way since the days when people feared them and did not want to mention their names. Today, fairies are seen as more benevolent and are sought out. Their images decorate people's homes. People read fantasy novels and watch films with fairy characters, and they attend workshops on how to see and communicate with fairies.

Humans are seeking a closer relationship with fairies, whoever they are, as part of a greater desire to explore the hidden realms of spirit. People are looking for ways to put magic and awe back into their lives.

Ted Andrews, a metaphysical teacher and author, observed that there is no big mystical secret to living a magical life. It cannot be obtained through spells, rituals, and incantations. The magical life happens when we let our inner child out to play, to be fully a part of the world around us. The doorways to the invisible realms never go away, nor do the fairies and elves.

"Our lives are surrounded and permeated by the awesome power of nature," said Andrews. "We have the choice to work with it and create or separate ourselves from it and destroy. The choice is ours."[4]

pounds. Huge stalks of broccoli were too heavy to lift from the ground. Local farmers were astonished. Agricultural experts, who examined the produce and the soil, could not explain their success.

The Caddys and Maclean publicized their spiritual partnership, and soon people from all over the world came to Findhorn to experience the magic for themselves. Findhorn boomed as a spiritual community.

During the 1970s, Findhorn had its ups and downs, and in 1980, Peter and Eileen went their separate ways. Eileen stayed on at Findhorn. Peter went to Europe. He died in a car accident in 1994. Maclean eventually settled in America, where she teamed up with David Spangler, a visionary who spent time at Findhorn, and others who are engaged in "re-visioning" the earth. Findhorn carries on under new management.

According to Maclean, the devas are the "builders" of the world, holding the energy patterns from which all things in nature spring into being. The devas told her that they are quite willing to work with humans, but humans must ask for their help. Otherwise, they cannot intervene. They emphasize the need to approach everything with love, which opens the door to knowledge of the unity of all things.

A NEW DIRECTION

Communities such as these have established a new frontier in the relationship between human beings and the residents of nature, including fairies and elementals. In the past, the relationship was tense and often unhappy. It seemed that people were at odds with fairies.

Today, a spirit of cooperation exists. Many individuals have their own miniature versions of Findhorn, right in their own backyards, and in the little herb gardens kept on city windowsills.

Can fairies help humans improve the environment and benefit the earth? Believe—and find out.

Timeline

1100s The Green Children are found in Woolpit, Suffolk, England

1200s Thomas the Rhymer spends seven years in Elfland, then is returned to earth and continues on as a consultant to the fairies

1645 Ann Jeffries fairy abduction case occurs in England

1692 Reverend Robert Kirk visits Fairyland and records his experiences in a diary

June 21, 1692 Kirk collapses near a fairy howe and dies the same night at home; he is rumored to have gone to Fairyland

1800s Authors record fairy folklore and stories in collections of fairy tales

1907–1911 W.Y. Evans-Wentz travels around the British Isles and France documenting fairy folklore and experiences

1917–1920s Cottingley Fairies hoax occurs in Yorkshire, England

1960s Findhorn is founded in Scotland

1970s-1980s More communities like Findhorn are founded

September 1979 Children play with fairies driving little cars in Nottingham, England

1980s Ufologists and folklorists study the similarities between extraterrestrials and fairies

1997 The story of the Cottingley Fairy Hoax is released in the film *Fairy Tale: A True Story*

March–April 2007 Artist Dan Baines claimed to have found the mummified remains of a fairy, which he photographed and displayed on the Internet; people around the world viewed the realistic fairy remains, which Baines revealed as a prank on April 1; he later sold the fairy sculpture on eBay

Glossary

BANSHEE A death omen fairy that wails and moans to forecast the death of a person.

BROWNIE A fairy that lives in human households and helps with chores.

CHANGELING A fairy baby or child substituted for a kidnapped human one.

DEVA Sanskrit term meaning "shining one," sometimes used to describe nature spirits.

DWARF A fairy that looks like a small, grotesque-shaped man. Dwarfs are excellent thieves.

ELEMENTAL A nature spirit associated with the four elements of earth, air, fire, and water. Elementals are sometimes defined as a type of fairy.

ELF Small beings that live in a middle realm. Some are good and some are evil.

ELF-SHOT Poisonous fairy arrows fatal to humans and animals; also, the condition of being shot with a fairy arrow.

FAERIE Spelling preferred by some people over "fairy." "Fae-rie" was used in earlier times to mean a state of enchantment.

FAIRY A wide variety of beings that populate an unseen realm close to earth. "Fairy" comes from the Latin term *fata*, or "fate." Fairies live in their own societies, usually accessed through the earth. Some tend nature and the elements.

FAIRY GODMOTHER A female fairy that looks after children and bestows blessings on a household.

FAIRY SIGHT See SIGHT.

GLAMOUR   A state of enchantment cast over mortals by fairies and witches that causes people to see and do whatever is commanded of them.

HOWE   A term for a FAIRY MOUND, a doorway between the human world and the fairy world.

IGNIS FATUUS   Latin term for "foolish fire," used to describe a wide variety of trickster fairies and spirits that look like moving balls of light or fire in the darkness. It is foolish to follow them. See WILL-O-THE-WISP.

KELPIE   A water fairy that attacks travelers and drowns them.

KOBOLD   A fairy that works in mines and is a metal smith.

KNOWE   See HOWE.

LEPRECHAUN   A solitary fairy that works as a shoemaker and guards hidden treasure, especially at the end of rainbows.

NATURE SPIRIT   A being, often described as a fairy, that tends things in nature and helps them grow.

PIXIE/PIXY   A fairy in Cornish lore that is mischievous and likes to lead travelers astray.

RADE   A solemn ride or procession of fairies, by foot and by fairy horse.

RATH   An Irish term for a fairy mound.

SEA DRAUG   In Scandinavian lore, a dreadful, evil fairy, similar to the SLUAGH, that flies about at night looking for mortals to attack.

SEELIE COURT   The good and kind fairies. "Seelie" is the Scottish Highland term for "blessed."

SIGHT   Clairvoyance, or the ability to see invisible spirits such as fairies, and their realms. People with sight also can see into the future.

SLUAGH   The Host or the Unforgiven Dead in Scottish Highland lore. "Sluagh" is pronounced "sloos." These evil, ill-tempered fairies are the spirits of malicious dead people, or fallen angels.

TEIND   A tithe fairies must pay the devil every seven years. The tithe might be a fairy or one of their mortal captives. The term comes from the Scottish Lowlands.

TROLL   In Scandinavian lore, an ugly fairy that lives beneath bridges. Some trolls are mean and attack travelers. Others amass great wealth.

UNSEELIE COURT   Bad, ill-tempered, and evil fairies that seek to harm people. "Unseelie" means "unblessed." See SEELIE COURT.

WILD HUNT   A band of fairies, witches, demons, hellhounds, and pagan gods and goddesses that rides the skies at night.

WILL-O-THE-WISP   A type of mischievous fairy that usually appears as a bobbing light in the darkness and leads travelers astray.

Endnotes

CHAPTER 1

1. Janet Bord. *Fairies: Real Encounters with Little People* (New York: Carroll & Graf Publishers, 1997), 126–128.

2. Rosemary Ellen Guiley. *The Encyclopedia of Magic and Alchemy* (New York: Facts On File, 2006), 97.

3. John Matthews. *The Secret Lives of Elves & Fairies: From the Private Journal of the Rev. Robert Kirk* (New York: Metro Books, 2006), 49.

4. Bord, 64–65.

5. Ibid., 68.

CHAPTER 2

1. William Martin. "Collecteana III In the Isle of Man," *Folk-Lore*, vol. 3 (1902): 186.

2. William Henderson. *Folk-lore of the Northern Counties* (London: Folklore Society, 1879), 253–55.

3. "True Mystic Experiences," *FATE* (May 1977): 52–53.

4. Karen Maralee. "Fairy Dust," *FATE* (September 1994): 55–56.

5. Dora Van Gelder. *The Real World of Fairies* (Wheaton, Ill.: The Theosophical Publishing House, 1977), 63.

CHAPTER 3

1. Katharine Briggs. *An Encyclopedia of Fairies: Hobgoblins, Brownies, Bogles and Other Supernatural Creatures* (New York: Pantheon Books, 1976), 394–95.

2. Ibid., 239–41.

3. John Matthews. *The Secret Lives of Elves & Fairies: From the Private Journal of the Rev. Robert Kirk.* (New York: Metro Books, 2005), 17.

CHAPTER 4

1. W.Y. Evans-Wentz. *The Fairy Faith in Celtic Countries.* (New York: Carroll Publishing Group, 1990), 149.

2. Briggs, 159–160.

3. W.B. Yeats. *The Celtic Twilight: Men and Women, Ghouls and Faeries.* (London: Lawrence & Bullen, 1893), 93.

4. D.A. McManus. *The Middle Kingdom: The Faerie World of Ireland* (London: Max Parrish, 1959), 62–63.

5. W. Jenkyn Thomas. "A Fairy Dog." *The Welsh Fairy Book.* Available online. URL: http://www.sacredtexts.com/neu/celt/wfb/wfb60.htm. Accessed June 11, 2009.

6. Evans-Wentz, 131.

7. Matthews, 97.

8. Katherine Briggs. *The Vanishing People* (New York: Pantheon Books, 1978), 174–175.

9. Evans-Wentz, 82.

10. Gordon Creighton. "A Weird Case from the Past," *Flying Saucer Review* 16, 4 (July/August 1970): 30.

11. Bord, 57.

12. McManus, 103.

CHAPTER 5

1. Thomas Keightley. *The World Guide to Gnomes, Fairies, Elves and Other Little People* (New York: Gramercy Books, 1978), 275–276.

2. Briggs, *The Vanishing People*, 118.

3. Ibid., 130–131.

4. Matthews, 82–84.

5. Rosemary Ellen Guiley. *The Encyclopedia of Witches, Witchcraft and Wicca*, 3d ed. (New York: Facts On File, 2008), 144.

6. Rosemary Guiley. *Fairy Magic*. (London: Element/Thorsons, 2004), 73–75.

CHAPTER 6

1. Reidar T. Christiansen, ed. "Folktales of Norway," in *Folk Tales of the World*. (Chicago: University of Chicago Press 1964), 53–54.

2. Guiley. *The Encyclopedia of Witches, Witchcraft and Wicca*, 360.

3. Briggs, *The Vanishing People*, 151.

4. Evans-Wentz, 109.

5. Rosemary Ellen Guiley, *Encyclopedia of Ghosts and Spirits*. (New York: Facts On File, 2008), 244–245.

6. Briggs, *Encyclopedia of Fairies*, 246.

7. Guiley, *Encyclopedia of Ghosts and Spirits*, 262.

8. Rosemary Ellen Guiley. *The Encyclopedia of Vampires, Werewolves and Other Monsters*. (New York: Facts On File, 2005), 240.

9. Briggs, *Encyclopedia of Fairies*, 20.

CHAPTER 7

1. Briggs, *The Vanishing People*, 101–102.

2. Evans-Wentz, 212.

3. Keightley, 232.

4. J.F. Campbell. *Popular Tales of the West Highlands*, vol. II (London: Alexander Gardner, 1890–93), 57–60.

5. Evans-Wentz, 198–199.

CHAPTER 8

1. Bord, 81–82.

2. Edwin Stanley Hartland. *Blows Against The Empire-The ET Hypothesis Comes Under Attack In UFOs, Time Slips, Other Realms and the Science of Fairies*. (New York: Global Communications, 2008), 10.

3. Jacques Vallee. *Passport to Magonia: On UFOs, Folklore and Parallel Worlds*. (New York: Contemporary Books, 1993), 41.

4. Ibid., 32–33.

5. Bob Pratt. *UFO Danger Zone: Terror and Death in Brazil—Where Next?* (Madison, Wisc.: Horus House Press, 1996), 55–56.

6. Vallee, 49.

CHAPTER **9**

1. Personal communication to author.
2. Guiley, *Fairy Magic*, 13–14.
3. Personal communication to author.
4. William Bloom. *Working with Angels, Fairies & Nature Spirits* (London: Piatkus, 1998), 74–75.

CHAPTER **10**

1. Rosemary Guiley, "Behold the Kingdom of the Nature Gods," *FATE* (June 1994): 17.
2. Ibid., 19.
3. Dorothy Maclean. *To Hear the Angels Sing.* (Hudson, N.Y.: Lindisfarne Press, 1980), 47.
4. Ted Andrews. *Enchantment of the Faerie Realm: Communicate with Nature Spirits & Elementals.* (St. Paul: Llewellyn Publications, 1996), 205.

Bibliography

Andrews, Ted. *Enchantment of the Faerie Realm: Communicate with Nature Spirits & Elementals*. St. Paul: Llewellyn Publications, 1996.

Bloom, William. *Working with Angels, Fairies & Nature Spirits*. London: Piatkus, 1998.

Bord, Janet. *Fairies: Real Encounters with Little People*. New York: Carroll & Graf Publishers, 1997.

Briggs, Katharine. *An Encyclopedia of Fairies: Hobgoblins, Brownies, Bogles and Other Supernatural Creatures*. New York: Pantheon Books, 1976.

Briggs, Katharine. *The Vanishing People*. New York: Pantheon Books, 1978.

Campbell, J.F. *Popular Tales of the West Highlands*. London, 1890–93.

Doyle, Sir Arthur Conan. *The Coming of the Fairies*. London: Hodder & Stoughton, 1922.

Evans-Wentz, W.Y. *The Fairy Faith in Celtic Countries*. New York: Carroll Publishing Group, 1990. First published 1911.

Ferm, Vergilius. *A Brief Dictionary of American Superstitions*. New York: Philosophical Library, 1965.

Guiley, Rosemary. *Fairy Magic*. London: Element/Thorsons, 2004.

Guiley, Rosemary Ellen. *The Encyclopedia of Magic and Alchemy*. New York: Facts On File, 2007.

Guiley, Rosemary Ellen. *The Encyclopedia of Witches, Witchcraft & Wicca*, 3d ed. New York: Facts On File, 2008.

Hartland, Edwin Stanley. *Blows Against The Empire—The ET Hypothesis Comes Under Attack In UFOs, Time Slips, Other Realms and the Science of Fairies*. New York: Global Communications, 2008.

Hodson, Geoffrey. *Fairies at Work and Play*. Wheaton, Ill.: Quest Books, 1982.

Keightley, Thomas. *The World Guide to Gnomes, Fairies, Elves and Other Little People*. New York: Gramercy Books, 1978. (First published in 1880 as *The Fairy Mythology*.)

Maclean, Dorothy. *To Hear the Angels Sing*. Hudson, N.Y.: Lindisfarne Press, 1980.

Matthews, John. *The Secret Lives of Elves & Fairies: From the Private Journal of the Rev. Robert Kirk*. New York: Metro Books, 2005.

McManus, D.A. *The Middle Kingdom: The Faerie World of Ireland*. London: Max Parrish, 1959.

Pratt, Bob. *UFO Danger Zone: Terror and Death in Brazil–Where Next?* Madison, Wisc.: Horus House Press, 1996.

Stewart, R.J. *The Living World of Faery*. Lake Toxaway, N.C.: Mercury Publishing, 1995.

Van Gelder, Dora. *The Real World of Fairies*. Wheaton, Ill.: The Theosophical Publishing House, 1977.

Vallee, Jacques. *Passport to Magonia: On UFOs, Folklore and Parallel Worlds*. New York: Contemporary Books, 1993.

Yeats, W.B. *The Celtic Twilight: Men and Women, Ghouls and Faeries*. London: Lawrence & Bullen, 1893.

Yeats, W.B. *Irish Fairy and Folk Tales*. London: Walter Scott, 1893.

Further Resources

Faerie

http://www.faeriemagazine.com/

A lavish, four-color quarterly magazine featuring articles about fairies
and works by leading artists.

Facrieworlds

http://www.faerieworlds.com/

Information about one of the largest annual outdoor festivals celebrating fairies. A family event, there are many activities for children
and youths as well as adults.

World of Froud

http://www.worldoffroud.com/index.html

Fairy art, stories, and news by leading fairy artists Brian and Wendy
Froud.

Fairies World

http://www.fairiesworld.com/

Extensive resources of literature, games, poems, art, events, Twitter,
and more.

Green Hope Farm

http://www.greenhopeessences.com/index.html

Molly Sheehan, founder of Green Hope Farm, tells the history or her
work with angels and devas, their gardening projects, and their
products. An archive of articles about the farm makes interesting
browsing.

Findhorn

http://www.findhorn.org/index.php?tz=240

The Findhorn community emphasizes spiritual growth and sustainable farming rather than contact with fairies. Nonetheless Findhorn exists and developed from the founders' work with fairy/deva cooperation.

Perelandra

http://www.perelandra-ltd.com/

Articles, products, resources, newsletters, and links to downloads are available.

Passport to Magonia

http://digitalseance.wordpress.com/2008/03/12/passport-to-magonia/

Ufologist Jacques Vallee's important study comparing extraterrestrials to fairies and other mysterious beings is available for free download.

Index

Page numbers in *italics* denote images.

About the Author
and
Consulting Editor

ROSEMARY ELLEN GUILEY is one of the foremost authorities on the paranormal. Psychic experiences in childhood led to her lifelong study and research of paranormal mysteries. A journalist by training, she has worked full time in the paranormal since 1983, as an author, presenter, and investigator. She has written 41 nonfiction books on paranormal topics, translated into 14 languages, and hundreds of articles. She has experienced many of the phenomena she has researched. She has appeared on numerous television, documentary, and radio shows. She is a columnist for *TAPS Paramagazine*, and a consulting editor for *FATE* magazine. Ms. Guiley's books include *The Encyclopedia of Angels*; *The Encyclopedia of Magic and Alchemy*; *The Encyclopedia of Saints*; *The Encyclopedia of Vampires, Werewolves, and Other Monsters*; and *The Encyclopedia of Witches, Witchcraft and Wicca*, all from Facts On File. She lives in Connecticut and her Web site is http://www.visionaryliving.com.